The Determinants and Consequences of Trade Restrictions in the U.S. Economy

THE DETERMINANTS AND CONSEQUENCES OF TRADE RESTRICTIONS IN THE U.S. ECONOMY

Victor A. Canto

PRAEGER SPECIAL STUDIES • PRAEGER SCIENTIFIC

New York • Philadelphia • Eastbourne, UK
Toronto • Hong Kong • Tokyo • Sydney

Library of Congress Cataloging-in-Publication Data

Canto, Victor A.
   The determinants and consequences of trade
restrictions in the U.S. economy.

   Bibliography: p.
   Includes index.
   1. Tariff—Law and legislation—United States.
2. Foreign trade regulation—United States.
3. United States—Economic policy—1981-
I. Title.
KF6659.C28   1985   382.7′0973   85-12211
ISBN 0-03-004964-4 (alk. paper)

Published in 1986 by Praeger Publishers
CBS Educational and Professional Publishing, a Division of CBS Inc.
521 Fifth Avenue, New York, NY 10175 USA

6789   052   987654321

Printed in the United States of America on acid-free paper

INTERNATIONAL OFFICES

Orders from outside the United States should be sent to the appropriate address listed below. Orders from areas not
listed below should be placed through CBS International Publishing, 383 Madison Ave., New York, NY 10175 USA

Australia, New Zealand
Holt Saunders, Pty. Ltd., 9 Waltham St., Artarmon, N.S.W. 2064, Sydney, Australia

Canada
Holt, Rinehart & Winston of Canada, 55 Horner Ave., Toronto, Ontario, Canada M8Z 4X6

Europe, the Middle East, & Africa
Holt Saunders, Ltd., 1 St. Anne's Road, Eastbourne, East Sussex, England BN21 3UN

Japan
Holt Saunders, Ltd., Ichibancho Central Building, 22-1 Ichibancho, 3rd Floor, Chiyodaku, Tokyo, Japan

Hong Kong, Southeast Asia
Holt Saunders Asia, Ltd., 10 Fl, Intercontinental Plaza, 94 Granville Road, Tsim Sha Tsui East, Kowloon,
Hong Kong

**Manuscript submissions should be sent to the Editorial Director, Praeger Publishers, 521 Fifth Avenue,
New York, NY 10175 USA**

To All the Girls I Love:

Ana Rosa, my wife;
Vianca Antonia, Victoria de Los Angeles, and Veronica Maria,
my daughters

Acknowledgments

During the last few years, I have been fortunate to participate in joint research with several of my colleagues. While this cooperation has greatly enhanced my productivity, it has also made it difficult to claim sole property rights to the projects and ideas that have emanated from the original research. This book is an example of a project whose origins can be traced to my interaction with several of my colleagues. Although I am claiming the property rights to this project, I feel justified in acknowledging several of my colleagues whose comments and suggestions have greatly enhanced the quality of this book. The list is headed by Art Laffer and Chuck Kadlec. Other people who have directly or indirectly contributed to the manuscript are: Kim Dietrich, Rich Eastin, Vishwa Mudaliar, Adish Jain, Marc Miles, and Jim Turney. Peggy Hansen and Ed Mooney read and edited parts of the manuscript. I would also like to thank Helen Pitts for typing the manuscript and B. J. Bickerton who proved to be a capable research assistant. Finally, I would like to thank Barbara Leffel for her encouragement and enthusiastic support.

Contents

List of Tables

List of Figures

The Determinants and Consequences of Trade Restrictions in the U.S. Economy

1
Historical Survey of U.S. Trade Policies*

INTRODUCTION

For the past 13 years, U.S. trade policy has been on a steady course toward increased protectionism. A policy to reduce tariffs across the board among all trading nations has been paralleled by efforts to protect selected industries from foreign competition. In the vernacular, the call for "free" trade has been joined by the admonition to seek "fair" trade. An increasing number of people have advocated protectionist policies in an effort to create a favorable balance of trade. Foreign competition increasingly is blamed for the decline in the health of the U.S. economy while problems of several of the economy's weakest sectors, including steel and autos, are attributed to an uncontrolled surge of imports.

The debate now is much the same as it was 200 years ago. Arguments today that favor increased protectionism incorporated several of the mercantilist concepts, including the importance of a positive trade balance to a nation's prosperity. By contrast, the economic principles invoked by those advocating free trade can be found in the writing of Adam Smith and his predecessors. The trade account is viewed as a means to provide consumers and producers with the widest possible access to foreign goods and markets. Though restrictions placed on trade by foreign nations can be harmful to the domestic economy, imposing additional restrictions on trade at the domestic level serves only to compound the loss of economic efficiency, limiting further the opportunities to realize the benefits of trade.

*V. A. Canto, "U.S. Trade Policy: History and Evidence," *The CATO Journal* vol. 3, no. 3, Winter 1983/1984 pages 679–698. Reprinted with permission.

The historical account of the U.S. trade policy presented in this chapter suggests that the rise of protectionist policies can be linked to the concern for the international competitiveness of U.S. products. The enthusiasm for restricting trade as a means to improve the domestic economy and protect selected industries, however, is tempered by the realization that trade restrictions can become counterproductive, impoverishing domestic and foreign producers and consumers alike.

HISTORICAL SURVEY OF U.S. TRADE POLICIES

The Trade Agreements Act of 1934

The roots of current U.S. trade policies can be traced back to the Trade Agreements Act of 1934. The purpose of this act, passed by the U.S. Congress, was to increase U.S. exports to foreign countries. There was a need for such an act for two reasons. First, the Hawley-Smoot Tariff Act of 1930 raised duties on imports to 53 percent in 1931 and 59 percent in 1932 (Fig.1.1). This action provoked other countries to retaliate against the United States, shrinking world trade. Second, the ensuing worldwide contraction in economic activity in the early 1930s caused world trade to decline even further. Between 1929 and 1933, world trade shrank 25 percent.

The Trade Agreements Act of 1934 delegated to the president the authority to negotiate U.S. trade agreements. It also allowed the president to participate in negotiations for the purpose of lowering tariffs to a level as low as 50 percent of the rates established by the Smoot-Hawley Act.

Extensions of the Trade Agreements Act, particularly after World War II, permitted the imposition of restrictions when harmful domestic effects could be shown to result from tariff cuts. Nevertheless, under the act, the United States signed bilateral trade agreements with 20 foreign nations. And, by 1947, tariff rates had been reduced to one-half their 1934 levels (Fig.1.1).

The General Agreement on Tariffs and Trade

In spite of this progress, it was apparent that, in the years preceding Wold War II, an alarming number of nations had adopted a neomercantilist, "beggar-thy-neighbor" approach to trade policy. Many politicians

FIGURE 1.1.   Effective Tax Rates on U.S. Imports 1929–78

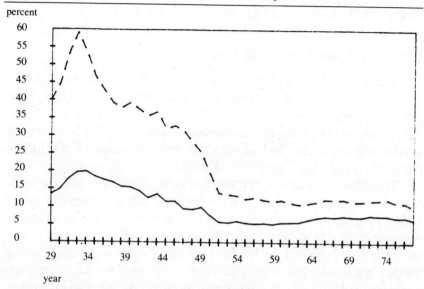

Source: National Income and Product Accounts of the United States, 1929–76, Statistical Tables, U.S. Department of Commerce.

and commentators specifically attributed the outbreak of war to that trade environment.

This feeling served as the underpinning for the major international efforts following the war in which open communication, free trade, and international economic interdependence were basic goals. Thus, the United Nations, the Bretton Woods agreement, and the General Agreement on Tariffs and Trade (GATT) were formed—all through the leadership of the United States.

GATT is particularly noteworthy for purposes of this study. It institutionalized the following basic goals:

1. Trade without discrimination (general, most-favored-nation treatment);
2. Protection of domestic industries only through tariffs;
3. Establishment of a predictable and stable basis for trade;
4. Consultation when trade problems arise;
5. Waivers and emergency actions that serve as exceptions to the general rules (e.g., escape clauses); and
6. Acceptance of regional trading arrangements.

Under the provisions of GATT, seven rounds of trade negotiations occurred: in 1947 (Geneva), 1949 (Annecy, France), 1951 (Torquay, England), 1956 (Geneva), 1961 (Dillon Round, Geneva), 1954 (Kennedy Round, Geneva), and 1975 (Tokyo Round, Geneva).

The Trade Expansion Act of 1962

During the span between 1947 and the mid-1950s, trade barriers were reduced on a commodity-by-commodity basis. After the mid-1950s, however, this method was considered ineffective for large-scale reductions. Participants in GATT therefore requested a "linear," or across-the-board, approach to tariff cuts. Such an approach was authorized when Congress passed the Trade Expansion Act of 1962.

The Trade Expansion Act was the most significant piece of trade legislation since the adoption of the Reciprocal Trade Agreements Act in 1934. This legislation was the statutory mandate for the president to negotiate tariff cuts at the next GATT-sponsored multilateral trade negotiations, later to be called the Kennedy Round. This act was significant for another reason: It established the office of the special trade representative (now the U.S. trade representative) to conduct the negotiations, replacing the State Department in this role. The purpose behind this shift was to meet congressional concerns that the State Department was too prone to negotiate trade agreements based on nebulous foreign policy grounds. Thus, trade policy was made less a stepchild of foreign policy and more subject to commercial realities and special-interest pressures.

The Kennedy Round

The Kennedy Round had three major objectives: (1) overall reduction in tariffs, (2) reduction of nontariff barriers, and (3) participation of less-developed countries. Of these three objectives, reduction of tariffs was the most successful. The reduction of nontariff barriers was not as successful as had been hoped.

Import duties were cut an average of 35 percent on manufactured goods and 20 percent on agricultural products (excluding cereals, meat, and dairy products). In all, about 70 percent of imported items were included in the cuts. By the end of the Kennedy Round, tariffs in the United States, the European Community, and Japan averaged only about 10 percent.

The Kennedy Round was also the first set of negotiations that addressed the problem of nontariff barriers, including:

1. Technical Barriers—mainly product standards, labeling and packaging restrictions, statements of origin, etc.;
2. Antidumping Policies—selling a product in a foreign market below the price charged by manufacturers in its home market or below cost;
3. The Government Procurement Code—regularizing the opening up procedures for government so that international sellers have better access to government contracts; and
4. The Customs Valuation Code—the evaluation of products for tariff purposes, nomenclature, and related customs procedures.

The inability of the participants to reach agreement in the reduction of nontariff barriers, however, anticipated many of the trade-related problems of the 1970s.

The Kennedy Round was concluded on June 30, 1967, when 53 nations signed agreements to put four years of negotiations into effect. The agreements were implemented over a five-year period ending in 1972. During the late 1960s, however, the steel and textile industries became primary advocates of restricting import competition. The Nixon administration responded to this pressure by endorsing textile and steel quotas. Also, the lack of international negotiations and the failure of GATT as an institution to resolve trade problems caused protectionist legislation to be introduced in Congress. While such legislation, epitomized by the Mills bill and the Burke-Hartke bill, never became law, it emphasized the growing pressure by special domestic interests to cope with the increasing pains of free trade and open-market policies.

New Forms of Trade Restraints

"Voluntary" Restraints

On January 1, 1969, the United States entered into voluntary restraint agreements with countries exporting all types of steel into the United States. Domestic manufacturers of steel called for these restraints because they feared injury from the tremendous increase of imported steel.[1] These restrictions were in effect until December 31, 1971. A second set of "voluntary" restraints were imposed January 1, 1972, which extended the restrictions until December 31, 1974.

President Nixon, in an effort to adhere to a 1968 campaign pledge, asked Japan and other countries to apply "voluntary" quotas on their exports of woolens and synthetic textiles to the United States. Because Japan was reluctant to abide by the "voluntary" quotas, the chairman of the House Ways and Means Committee, Wilbur Mills, with encouragement from the administration, introduced a bill in May 1969 to limit textile imports to their average annual level recorded in 1967 and 1968.

The Trade Bill of 1970

This action was a sharp departure from more than 30 years of U.S. leadership toward liberalizing trade. In the closed sessions that followed, the committee converted the president's bill into the most protectionist legislation since the Smoot-Hawley Act of 1930. It permitted any industry, when threatened by imports, to seek and obtain protection.

The bill was opposed by the European Economic Community. European governments threatened to retaliate if the bill became law. In spite of heavy opposition to the bill within the United States, especially among major exporters and multinationals, the House of Representatives passed it in November 1970. The Senate also appeared ready to pass the bill. But it adjourned before the vote could be taken, leaving the trade issue to be taken up anew by the next Congress as it convened in January 1971.[2]

The Burke-Hartke Bill

The near passage of the Trade Act of 1970 encouraged protectionist groups to seek even greater limits to free trade. Representative Burke and Senator Hartke placed a bill before Congress called the Foreign Trade and Investment Act of 1972, the Burke-Hartke bill. The objective of this bill was to provide for significant increases in government intrusion and regulation of the international flow of goods and capital. This bill was never passed, but it set the terms of trade debate for the first half of the decade.

The Burke-Hartke bill combined traditional protectionism (import restrictions) with new forms of protectionism, including restrictions on direct foreign investment. In addition, a foreign trade and investment commission, composed of three persons appointed by the president and confirmed by the Senate, would have been established. The commission would have been required to restrict imports to the average quantity for the period 1965–69. The commission's other responsibilities would have included estimating production schedules for various categories of goods from the previous year and fixing import quotas for each category and its supplying country. In order to grant an exception to these limits, the commission was supposed to act, in effect, as a central planning agency for the major sectors of the U.S. economy. The protectionist movement of Burke-Hartke would have frozen the 1967–69 ratio of imported goods to the production of "similar" domestic goods for an undetermined amount of time. It also attempted to freeze the geographic patterns of goods in each category.

The Demise of Bretton Woods

During this same period, the Bretton Woods agreement on international monetary policy collapsed. In August 1971, President Nixon, in violation of the Bretton Woods agreement, refused to convert dollars into gold for foreign central banks. The dollar was devalued 8.6 percent relative to gold, making the official price of an ounce of gold $38. Tariffs were increased across the board by 10 percent, and wage and price controls were imposed on the domestic economy. In December of that year, the tariff increase was rescinded and, under the Smithsonian agreement, the devaluation of the dollar against gold was "approved." A general realignment of currency values relative to the dollar also was established. The value of the dollar, however, remained under pressure. Gold convertibility was not restored. And, in February 1973, the United States devalued the dollar by another 10 percent relative to gold and, implicitly, relative to most foreign currencies as well.[3] In the months that followed, one country after another halted efforts to maintain a fixed exchange rate with the dollar, ushering in the present system of floating exchange rates. Efforts to restore dollar/gold convertibility ceased.

The fracturing of the international monetary system and the shift in the trade debate toward extreme protectionism represented by the Burke-Hartke bill paved the way for advocates of selective limits on foreign competition to appear moderate and constructive.

The Trade Act of 1974

The Trade Act of 1974 provided the broadest congressional mandate in history for the conduct of trade negotiations regarding the reduction of both tariff and nontariff barriers. The president was authorized to reduce tariffs as much as 60 percent below the levels that prevailed at the close of the Kennedy Round. It also called upon the president to begin negotiations for the purpose of strengthening the GATT system so that it could serve the purpose that the multilateral negotiations had served: diffusing and resolving trade conflicts.

However, in response to industry and congressional pressure, the cost of this broad mandate was the adoption of several provisions that eased the criteria necessary for imposing trade restraints. These included more flexible criteria for relief from increasing (but "fair") import competition, as well as substantive and procedural revisions of unfair trade practice laws (such as the antidumping and countervailing duty statutes). Thus, in addressing problems created by import competition considered to be "fair" the Trade Act of 1974 provided that an industry no longer need demonstrate that its injury was caused by imports resulting from an earlier tariff concession or that imports are the "major" cause—i.e., a cause no less important than any other cause—of its injury. Under the 1974 Trade Act, an industry need only show that imports are a "substantial" cause. If the International Trade Commission (ITC) finds injury, the president then must consider what impact trade restrictions would have on the domestic economy, consumers, and the overall national interests. The final determination of what action, if any, should be taken is, essentially, at his descretion. The ITC may, however, recommend adjustment assistance instead of trade restrictions. If the president does not proclaim the relief recommended by the ITC, Congress may override the president and institute the relief recommended by the commission.

The authority of the president to impose quantity restrictions was increased: For the first time, the president was authorized to negotiate orderly marketing agreements as a form of relief under the escape clause. The act also required the fulfillment of reciprocity in trade concessions before a trade agreement could be binding between the United States and another major industrial country. The Trade Act of 1974 triggered a rash of demands by U.S. industries for relief from import competition. These included requests for antidumping and countervailing duties, as well as escape clause restrictions on such items as chemical products, steel products, consumer electronics, industrial fasteners, canned hams, and vinyl shoes.

Changes in tariff policies were specifically circumscribed by GATT.[4] The GATT agreements also sought to prohibit the use of quantitative restrictions, which were viewed as more harmful than tariffs. However, these prohibitions were not specific enough to prevent circumvention through quantitative restrictions that were quotas in all but name. Moreover, various kinds of nontariff barriers were introduced on a plethora of products. Among the most complex of these agreements were the multifiber arrangements, establishing the parameters for restricting textile imports by the industrialized countries (effective January 1, 1974).

The use of "voluntary export restraints" also expanded during the 1970s. Under this arrangement, the importing country negotiates an agreement with the exporting country for that country to limit "voluntarily" the amounts of certain exports. In the United States, such negotiated trade restrictions, in the form of orderly marketing agreements, have been imposed on speciality steels, color TV receivers, nonrubber footwear, certain meats, mushrooms, textiles, and automobiles. In 1976 the president obtained an orderly marketing agreement to limit specialty steel exports with Japan, and unilateral quotas were imposed on imports from the EEC and various countries.

The Tokyo Round

Under the Trade Act of 1974, the president entered into the Tokyo Round of Multilateral Trade Negotiations. Once again, tariff reductions were high on the agenda. But reduction of nontariff barriers also were considered an integral part of the negotiations. The agreements reached were signed in December 1978, and represented potential progress in both tariff and nontariff reductions.

Tariff reductions averaged about 30 percent for the United States, 22 percent for Japan, and 27 percent for the European Economic Community. Nontariff reductions centered on the codes discussed earlier but generally were attempts to make trade-barrier activities transparent and explicit rather than hidden. The tariff reductions centered on "harmonization," wherein higher tariffs are reduced by a higher percentage than lower tariffs. Agreement was achieved on the "Swiss formula" with exceptions made for particularly sensitive commodities.[5] Had the Swiss formula been applied in its strictest sense, tariff reductions on average would have been 41 percent for the United States, 43 percent for the EEC, 68 percent (in applied rates) for Japan, and 39 percent (in applied rates) for Canada.

Failure of the United States and other countries to meet the tariff reductions dictated by the Swiss formula created a general environment of tariff reduction avoidance. When concessions were made for one country, other countries felt it in their best interest to protect themselves by maintaining higher tariffs on items of particular sensitivity in their countries. Agreements affecting nontariff barriers were reached in three major areas: codes for conducting international trade, reform of the GATT framework, and the reductions of nontariff barriers in specific products.

Six codes were agreed upon in Geneva. They addressed such trade problems as government procurement, the use of export subsidies, the imposition of countervailing duties, "dumping" of goods in foreign markets, customs valuation, the setting of standards for imports, and the issuance of import licenses, In addition, two other codes were discussed but no agreement was reached. GATT allowed countries to protect themselves against import surges in order to safeguard domestic industries. But increasingly, major industrial nations ignored the GATT mechanisms and used bilateral negotiations that allowed countries to "voluntarily" limit their exports of industrial-threatening products.

RECENT DEVELOPMENTS

In March 1979, the U.S. international Trade Commission determined that Korean bicycle tires and tube imports were injuring domestic producers.[6] In October, the ITC recommended that President Carter impose three years of quotas on Russian anhydrous ammonia. In November, the commission proposed a sharp increase in U.S. import duties on low-priced procelain and on steel cookware. By late spring of 1980, pressure was building to impose significantly higher import duties on small trucks imported from Japan. In August 1980, that pressure resulted in a 25 percent duty on lightweight truck chassis originating in Japan.[7]

A significant increase in the use of trade restrictions as a foreign policy weapon was witnessed in 1980.[8] In response to the Soviet invasion of Afghanistan, the United States forbade domestic exporters to sell corn, wheat, and certain fertilizer products to the Soviet Union. Severe restrictions also were placed on the export of high technology products.

In the summer of 1980, Ford Motor Company joined with the United Auto Workers to petition the ITC to grant protection from import competition from Japan. The U.S. International Trade Commission determined that imports were not a substantial cause of the domestic auto industry's sales problem. But Congress and the executive branch responded to political pressure and "voluntary" export restraints were discussed with the Japanese government. In effect, the Japanese automakers agreed—under pressure from the Japanese government—to restrict exports to the United States to 1.68 million units in the year following April 1981, and not to increase their exports unless the U.S. sales of all autos expand.

Although the Reagan administration endorses free trade, it is considering a new trade policy based on "reciprocity." The goal is to force other industrial nations to reduce their trade barriers to American-made goods and to reduce subsidies to their export industries. If a nation fails to meet these conditions, special restrictions and/or tariffs conceivably would be imposed on its exports to the United States.

The approach represents a radical change in U.S. trade policy. In essence, it is a bilateral framework that requires negotiations with all countries that trade with the United States before extension of the U.S. most-favored-nation (minimum) tariff structure. This policy would represent an abandonment of the unconditional most-favored-nation principle that has been the foundation of trade policy among the industrial nations since 1933. As such, it invites increased protectionism among the industrial countries, and threatens a return to the "beggar-thy-neighbor" policies of the early 1930s.

The move toward protectionism got another push when the domestic steel industry on January 11, 1982 filed forms with the Commerce Department and the International Trade Commission charging nine European countries, Brazil, and South Africa with unfair trade practices. In its preliminary rulings, the Commerce Department found that nine foreign governments had been unfairly subsidizing steel exports. The International Trade Commission agreed that 90 percent of the unfair trade complaints represented reasonable injury to domestic steel products. The Commerce Department's final ruling reduced most of the subsidy margins cited in its preliminary determination and narrowed the list of offenders to six Western European countries.

On October 21, just hours before the Commerce Department would have been required to impose countervailing and penalty duties—selective increases in U.S. tariffs and duties—quota negotiations were finalized limiting European steel imports to about 85 percent of 1981 levels. In addition, the quotas were extended to pipe and tube products. The accord has two parts:

1. Carbon and alloy steel shipments will be limited to an average 5.44 percent of the projected U.S. market. The pact also sets individual ceilings for specific categories. The Europeans will set up a new export licensing system to enforce this part of the accord.
2. Pipe and tube exports will be restricted to 5.9 percent of expected U.S. demand. If it seems likely that the limit will be breached, the two sides will have 60 days to find a settlement. Otherwise, either may impose new restrictions.

The United States will help enforce the agreement by invoking a newly enacted law that allows the customs service to block specified steel imports that have not received foreign export licenses. Such actions could undercut U.S. efforts to persuade the Western Europeans and Japanese to move toward freer trade by dropping some nontariff barriers.

Restrictions on U.S. exports to the Soviet Union and U.S. efforts to curtail East-West trade in the aftermath of martial law in Poland also threaten to disrupt trading patterns that have been established during the past 10 years. That, too, will detract from economic growth both in Western Europe and Japan, increasing economic tensions among the industrial countries.

With record trade deficits persisting, implementation of the new GATT codes of conduct only beginning, and unemployment rates in the United States near their postwar high, pressure will be intense to protect American industries, from autos and steel to textiles and footwear. The influence of the protectionist groups is fairly apparent in the various trade legislation currently on Congress' agenda. The influence of protectionist groups is felt both in the formulation of protectionist legislation and free trade policies. An example of the push for protectionism on Capitol Hill is the local content legislation that is aimed at largely eliminating Japanese auto imports. Protectionist influence is also evident in the supposedly "free trade" type of legislation such as the Carribean Basin Initiative. This legislation would reduce trade barriers for numerous commodities but retain protection for textiles and sugarcane—commodities in which the Carribean region has a clear comparative advantage.[9]

The November 1982 GATT Meeting

In November 1982, for the first time since 1973, a GATT ministerial meeting was held. The following major issues appeared on the GATT agenda:[10]

1. A moratorium on protectionism, designed to stem the proliferation of new trade barriers;
2. A new safeguards system that would limit the import restraints a country may impose to protect industries threatened by foreign competition;
3. Extension of the GATT rules to cover trade in services, investments, and high-technology products;
4. Common Market subsidies on agricultural exports;
5. A proposed round of negotiations between rich and poor countries aimed at opening the developing countries; and
6. The development of a dispute-settling mechanism.

One of the objectives of the meeting was to reassure the world that the majority trading countries would resist the kind of protectionism that could result in a worsened worldwide recession. However, due to the dis-agreement among member countries, the meetings were doomed to fail-ure.[11] Even the GATT director doubted that much agreement could be reached on the major issues, such as import safeguards.[12]

At best, the results of the ministerial meeting can be considered a symbolic victory for free trade. The member countries committed them-selves in principle to avoid further violations of GATT rules and to cor-rect existing ones. The document, however, lacks any new measures to reinforce that pledge.[13]

The lack of agreement on the major policy issues discussed at the GATT ministerial session should not be surprising to an economist. The dismantling, as well as the imposition, of trade restrictions alters the in-centive structure of different interest groups in the member countries. The restrictions clearly increase the well-being of some of the poor member countries. However, to the extent that the restrictions do not benefit the world as a whole, countries negatively affected will either try to circum-vent the regulations[14] or lobby for more favorable restrictions.[15]

Trade restrictions give rise to economic rents. This in turn gives rise to rent-seeking behavior. To the extent that those countries that benefit from the actions can organize effectively, the political process may re-sult in protectionist policies.[16] Thus one of the problems for advocates of free trade is to keep protectionist pressures within bounds and to avoid repeating the experience of the Smoot-Hawley Act of 1930.[17]

The Williamsburg Summit

Recent developments are not encouraging to those who advocate free trade. At first glance, the trade restrictions of high tariffs and new quotas on specialty steel and an effective increase in tariffs on frozen concen-trated orange juice from Brazil seem too superficial to be concerned about. But a close look reveals that the threat posed by the restrictions is poten-tially far more than a mere blemish on the economic recovery of the world economy. The actions suggest a retaliatory behavior on the part of the United States. This view becomes more credible as one takes into con-sideration the fact that the countries affected were the ones opposed to the major issues discussed at the November 1982 GATT meeting.

The decision by the president to provide protection to the specialty steel industry, little more than a month after the May 1983 Williamsburg economic summit, undercuts the U.S. efforts to ease trade barriers among the industrialized countries. To add insult to injury, the new restrictions on steel—ranging from higher tariffs on stainless steel sheet strips and plates to quotas on stainless steel bars and plates, and alloy tool steel products, which reduce imports by as much as 44 percent below their 1983 levels—fall largely on six industrial nations: Canada, France, West Germany, Italy, Japan, and the United Kingdom.

Administration arguments that the new trade restrictions are designed to foster the goals of the Williamsburg summit by pressuring other nations to get rid of practices injuring U.S. producers are fatuous. The European response was to threaten retaliation with higher tariffs on U.S. exports to the Common Market. Furthermore, the U.S. actions ignored recent European moves reducing "unfair" trade practices. Prior to the economic summit, the Common Market countries had agreed to phase out, over the next 18 months, the steel subsidies that are so offensive to U.S. producers and the administration. Yet, the higher tariffs and quotas will prevail for four years.

THE NEAR-TERM OUTLOOK FOR TRADE RESTRICTIONS

Recently, the momentum for protectionist measures has increased to dangerous levels. At the London summit, leaders of the industrial world failed to agree even to begin another round of trade negotiations aimed at reducing trade barriers.

At home, the shoe industry's petition was denied, and fishing talks between Canada and the U.S. were ended without agreement. But the ITC has ruled that both the steel and copper industries have been "injured" by imports. As a result the President was forced to rule on a new round of import barriers. President Reagan's action on steel import quotas had all the makings of another decision that would impact policy for years to come. The immediate stakes seemed narrowed: The U.S. International Trade Commission (ITC) had recommended that import quotas and additional tariffs be imposed on foreign steel in five major steel product areas for the next five years. This protection from foreign competition would be contingent upon the domestic steel industry's demonstrating a willingness to reduce costs, including wages, and to modernize its facilities. But the scope of the proposal indicated that the tone, if not the substance, of trade policy for the remainder of the decade might well be established by Reagan's ruling on the ITC recommendation.

- For the first time, quotas would be imposed upon all foreign steel. Previously, limits on foreign steel had been imposed on a country-by-country basis.

- Steel's role as a major raw material input, and as a significant factor in world trade, suggests that the ramifications of the steel decision extend well beyond the domestic steel industry.
- For the first time, trade restrictions were being linked directly to periodic government review and approval of the industry's "rehabilitation" program. Such supervision is far from benign and can easily turn malignant. It increases the government's role in making important economic decisions and raises the stakes government officials have in the program's success or failure. The problem is that government rarely faces up to failure, and even less frequently achieves success when attempting to bail out an inefficient industry.

More alarming is the passage of the Simpson-Mazzoli bill, a clear sign of the strength of protectionist sentiment in Congress. Parallels between this bill and trade restrictions are precise. Simpson-Mazzoli purports to save jobs and strengthen the U.S. economy by restricting the flow of workers—referred to in the pejorative as "illegal aliens"—into the U.S. Trade restrictions seek to limit the flow of goods into the U.S. Both restrictions are, with rare exceptions, counterproductive. Undocumented workers do not destroy jobs. The supply of their work effort to the economy is equal to their demand for goods and services. Illegal aliens working in this country do so in order to acquire goods and services. Consequently, as many jobs are created by their presence in this country as are taken.

A fourth sign of increasing momentum for protectionism is the unsolicited support by Chrysler Chairman Lee Iacocca for steel import quotas. In a letter to Representative Sam Gibbons (D-FL.), Chairman of the House Ways and Means Committee trade subcommittee, Iacocca said that legislation that would limit steel imports was needed to "insure the long-term health of the steel, automaking, and other basic industries."[18] However, limiting Chrysler's access to inexpensive foreign steel can only diminish its capacity to compete with foreign automakers that have access to a lower cost raw material. The apparent agenda, therefore, is to support the efforts to restrict that industry's foreign competitors in the hope of gaining the steel industry's support for similar auto import restrictions.

CONCLUSION

In the name of free trade, the administration is considering a new trade policy based on "reciprocity." The goal is to force other nations to reduce their trade barriers to American-made goods and to reduce subsidies to their export industries. If a nation fails to meet this condition, the U.S. response may be to impose restrictions and/or tariffs on their exports to the U.S.

The policy issue thus centers on whether judiciously applied protectionist measures can contribute to domestic economic stability and growth. In particular, can instruments of trade policy be used to improve a country's balance of trade and thus its overall economic performance? Furthermore, can specific industries suffering from import competition be assisted through protectionist measures, thereby reducing unemployment and increasing total output and income?

The "reciprocity" approach represents a radical change in policy. In essence, it is a bilateral framework that requires negotiations with all countries before extension of the U.S. most-favored-nation (minimum) tariff structure. This policy would represent an abandonment of the unconditional most-favored-nation principle that has been the foundation of trade policy among the industrial nations since 1933. By putting trade negotiations back into a bilateral framework, the reciprocity approach invites increased protectionism among the industrial countries, thus threatening a return to the "beggar-thy-neighbor" policies of the early 1930s. Reciprocity is just the latest step in the steady drift in U.S. policy away from free trade.

Advances toward free trade have been at least partially offset with increases in nontariff barriers as the free trade policies began to conflict with a growing protectionist sentiment in the U.S. A review of major U.S. trade actions indicates a steady reduction in tariffs throughout the 1934–81 period (Table 1.1). An example of the dichotomy between restricting and freeing trade is the requirement that domestic industries for the first time show material injury by subsidized imports before countervailing duty would be imposed. Previously, the evidence of foreign subsidies was the only requirement for imposition of the tariffs. But the Act also requires the President to determine that the foreign country had become a signatory of the Tokyo Round agreements and accepted a similar obligation vis-à-vis the U.S. Otherwise, this additional protection to trade granted under the Tokyo Round does not apply.

The grim experience of the early 1930s amply demonstrates that this movement toward protectionism carries with it major implications for the U.S. economy. Virtually all economists and policymakers agree that, in the extreme, trade restrictions are self-defeating, impoverishing foreign countries and U.S. citizens alike.

Ironically, the growing push for protectionism is due, in part, to the success of the Reagan administration's economic program. Pressures for trade restrictions typically rise when the trade balance deteriorates. And, a country's trade balance tends to deteriorate when its economy grows faster than the rest of the world's. When a country is growing at an above-average rate, it tends to acquire more goods and services (consumption) and capital goods (investment) than it produces. The difference is net imports from the rest of the world as foreign suppliers provide the excess goods, services, and capital goods in exchange for future claims (bonds and stocks) against the output of the U.S. economy.

TABLE 1.1. Summary of U.S. Major Trade Actions (1930–82)

Free Trade Activities	*Protectionist Activities*
Trade Agreement Act of 1934 (President given the authority to negotiate U.S. trade policy and reduce specific tariffs up to 50 percent).	Smoot-Hawley Tariff Act of 1930 (raised duties upon agricultural raw materials from 38 percent to 49 percent and on other commodities from 31 percent to 34 percent, with special protection given to sugar and textile interests).
General Agreement on Tariffs and Trade: (1) Geneva, October 1947; GATT was concluded by 28 nations, with some two thirds of trade items between the participating countries covered by concessions;	The Federal Buy American Act of 1933. (Requires federal agencies purchasing commodities for use within the United States to pay up to a 6 percent differential for domestically produced products).
(2) Annecy, France, 1949, additional countries entered the Geneva Agreement and the U.S. granted concessions on about 400 items.	Bilateral trade agreements signed with 20 nations reducing average tariffs to one-half their 1934 levels (1934–47).
General Agreement on Tariffs and Trade: (3) Torquay, England, September 1950 to April 1951; U.S. received concessions on an estimated half billion dollars of 1949 exports.	Agricultural Adjustment Act of 1935, section 22 (permits the president to regulate the imports of agricultural products if such imports materially interfere with the price support programs operated by the U.S. Department of Agriculture).
Trade Agreement Act extended for three years (authority granted to Eisenhower to reduce tariffs 5 percent a year in return for foreign concessions and reduce 5 percent those duties in excess of 50 percent ad valorem [1955]).	The Merchant Marine Act of 1936 (the "Jones Act") requires that all ocean-going shipments from one point in the United States to another be transported in U.S. flat vessels.
Trade Expansion Act of 1962 (President given authority to reduce tariffs of July 1, 1962, by 50 percent in 5 years; (1)	Agricultural Act of 1956 (authorizes President to negotiate with foreign governments to limit exports from such

TABLE 1.1. (*continued*)

Free Trade Activities	Protectionist Activities

allowed elimination of U.S. and European Economic Community together accounting for 80 percent of free world exports; (2) selected agricultural commodities where changes would assure some increase in U.S. exports of like goods; (3) tropical agricultural forestry products not produced in the U.S. if the European Economic Community would reciprocate; (4) articles which had an ad valorem rate of 5 percent).

The sixth GATT tariff conference (known as the Kennedy Round; authorized 50 percent tariff reductions on most industrial products and 30 percent to 50 percent on others; 1962).

President Johnson calls for abolition of American Selling Price (1968).

Implementation of Kennedy Round tariff reductions completed (1972).

Trade Act of 1974 (stimulate U.S. economic growth and maintain and enlarge some of the foreign markets for U.S. products; enhance economic relations with foreign countries through the development of open and nondiscriminatory trade in the free world).

Tokyo Round (attempted to constrain nontariff barriers; negotiations designed to liberalize international trade; 1975).

Specialty steel quota reductions begun— to be completed in 1980 (July 1979).

Orderly Market Agreement to restrict imports to color televisions with Japan allowed to lapse (1980).

Specialty steel quotas allowed to lapse (1980).

Embargoes on shipments to the Soviet

countries and imports into the United States of agricultural commodities).

Quota restrictions announced on imports of lead and zinc to 80 percent of average of preceding 5 years (1958).

Mandatory quotas on oil imports imposed (1950).

Trade Agreement Act extended (1958) for an additional four years; authorized increasing rates 50 percent above rates in effect on July 1, 1934, rather than on January 1, 1945.

Established voluntary quotas limiting the importation of cotton textiles (1961).

Raised tariffs on sheet glass and carpets (1962).

Price differential for defense procurement of foreign military goods raised to 50 percent (1962).

Meat Import Act of 1964 (designed to protect domestic cattle industry; quotas come into effect when imports exceed adjusted base by 10 percent [trigger level]; president may elect to suspend quotas).

The Interest Equalization Tax (designed to restrict the sale of foreign securities in the United States [1964]).

The Voluntary Foreign Credit Restraints Program (designed to restrict the availability to foreigners of banking services in the United States; mid-1960s).

Foreign Direct Investment Program (designed to restrict U.S. financing of foreign direct investments by U.S. firms; mid-1960s).

Informal restraints on major meat sup-

TABLE 1.1. (*continued*)

Free Trade Activities	*Protectionist Activities*
Union of wheat, superphosphoric acid, and other products ended (1981).	plying countries; special bilateral restrictions with Honduras (1969).
Orderly Marketing Agreement on non-rubber footwear expired (1981).	Nixon administration submits bill to restrict textile trade (1969).
Orderly Marketing Agreement to restrict imports of color televisions with Taiwan and S. Korea allowed to lapse (1982).	Voluntary Restraint Agreement imposed on imports of steel (1969).
Caribbean Basin Initiative proposed by the Reagan administration (1982).	Trade Act of 1970 passed by the House but defeated by the Senate (the most restrictive trade legislation since the Smoot-Hawley Tariff Act).
	Voluntary restraints on meat imports negotiated with additional countries (1970).
	Burke-Hartke bill introduced in Senate in 1971 (introduced new forms of protectionism).
	President Nixon orders the gold window closed and imposes an across-the-board 10 percent increase in tariffs (1971).
	Tariffs on stainless steel flatware raised (1971).
	Negotiated voluntary quotas on Mexican fruit and vegetables (1971).
	Price differential for defense procurement of foreign hand tools raised to 50 percent (1971).
	Restraint program on meat continued which allowed for 1971 imports to be higher than the suspended trigger level but below negotiated restraint levels (1971).
	Voluntary Restraint Agreement on steel extended from 1971 to 1974 (1972).
	Voluntary restraints negotiated on meat (1972).
	OPEC oil embargo (1973).

TABLE 1.1. (*continued*)

Free Trade Activities	Protectionist Activities
	U.S. soybean export embargo (1974).
	Trade Act of 1974 (provides safeguards for American industry and American workers for unfair or injurious import competition; provide "adjustment assistance" for industries or workers hurt by imports).
	Multifibre Arrangements—1974 (restricted textile imports).
	Tokyo Round—1975 (implementation of safeguards and protection from international trade).
	Voluntary restraint negotiated on meat (1975).
	Orderly Marketing Agreement negotiated with Korea and Taiwan to restrict imports of nonrubber footwear to 1976 levels.
	Quotas placed on specialty steel (1976).
	Orderly Marketing Agreement with Japan to restrict imports of color television (1977). Voluntary restrictions on meat imports negotiated; Canadian imports negotiated for first time.
	Trigger Price Mechanism on steel implemented (1978).
	Restraints on imports of industrial fasteners (after once failing at the ITC) were imposed; the Commission was required to consider it again following Ways and Means Committee request (1979).
	Trade Act of 1979 (overhauled U.S. countervailing duty laws which were designed to protect domestic industries against foreign government subsidies on imported goods; domestic industries required to show injury by subsidized im-

TABLE 1.1. (*continued*)

Free Trade Activities	Protectionist Activities
	ports before offsetting duty would be imposed; speeded investigations and imposition of penalties under countervailing duty and antidumping laws; established new customers valuation which used price actually paid for merchandise when sold for exportation to U.S.; discouraged discrimination against foreign suppliers bidding for government purchase; curbed use of standards as disguised trade barriers).
	Shipments to the Soviet Union of wheat, superphosphoric acid, and other products embargoed (1980).
	25 percent tariff imposed on lightweight chassis trucks (1980).
	"Voluntary" export restraint negotiated with Japan to restrict automobile imports (1980).
	Orderly Marketing Agreement with Korea and Taiwan to restrict imports of color televisions (1980).
	Embargoes on exports requiring validated licenses for shipment to Poland and the Soviet Union (1981).
	Renewal of Restrictions on Safeguards of copyrights of nondramatic literary publications (1982).
	Fair Practices in Automotive Products Act. Proposed legislation on local content laws (1982).
	Harley-Davidson seeks U.S. trade protection from Japanese imports (1982).

NOTES

1. See "The Attractions of Quotas," *Wall Street Journal.*
2. A discussion of the debate on the proposed legislation is contained in a series of staff articles in the *Wall Street Journal*, November 19-20, 1970.
3. For a discussion of the major trade issues at the time, see "U.S. Devalues 10% by Raising Price of Gold; Japan Agrees to Let Yen Float." *Wall Street Journal.*
4. GATT's Director General views on bilateral trade are detailed in Bahree (1981).
5. Specifically, the Swiss formula called for a tariff rate X to be reduced to a lower rate, Z, according to the formula $Z=4X/(X+14)$. This formula would result in larger percentage cuts for higher rates. There was no historical or intellectual reason for the choice of this particular formula. It was chosen principally because it was simple and implied an acceptable average of depth of cut.
6. See "U.S. Ruling Faults Imports of Korean Bicycle Tires," *Wall Street Journal.*
7. See Andy Pasztos (1980).
8. Support for these actions can be found in Allen (1980).
9. See G. Sieb (1982).
10. For a more detailed description of the basic issues, see Pine (1982a).
11. See Pine (1982b & c).
12. See World Briefs column in the *Wall Street Journal*, October 8, 1982.
13. See Pine (1982d).
14. For an analysis of individual behavior and smuggling in the presence of trade restriction, see Bhagwati and Hansen (1973), Bhagwati and Srinivasan (1973), and Falvey (1978).
15. For a discussion on the politics of special interest groups, see Brock and Magee (1978).
16. Analysis of the rent-seeking behavior can be traced to Krueger's (1974) seminal paper. Krueger's analysis has been further refined and generalized by Bhagwati and Srinivasan (1980).
17. On this issue, see Straus (1982).
18. "Chrysler Backs Steel Quota Bill," *New York Times.*

2
Developed Countries' Reaction to U.S. Trade Policies

THE NATURE OF U.S. TRADE POLICY

This chapter describes the reaction of the European Economic Community (EEC) and of Japan to changes in U.S. trade policy. The EEC and Japan have been selected for study for two reasons. First, these countries are the major trading partners of the United States; hence, their policies have a large impact on the U.S. economy. Second, a significant portion of the rest of the world, in particular many of the Less Developed Countries (LDC's), are not signatories of the General Agreement on Tariff and Trade (GATT). The diversity of economies and policies among non-GATT countries makes it extremely difficult to succinctly summarize these nations' responses to U.S. policies, although we do note one characteristic: Developing countries generally are more protectionist in their trade policy than are developed nations.

U.S. Trade Policy during the 1960s

U.S. trade policy during the postwar period was based primarily on the GATT guidelines. These guidelines, established in 1947, emphasized the principle of "trade without descrimination" and allowed for the protection of domestic industries solely through the use of tariffs. Across-the-board changes took the form of tariff reductions or increases within the GATT framework. However, the bulk of U.S. trade actions affecting individual products were implemented through quantity restrictions. Table 1.1 in Chapter 1 provides a summary of the major trade events of the postwar period.

23

The 1960s were dominated by the Kennedy Round of tariff negotiations. The major objective of the negotiation was overall reduction in tariff and nontariff barriers. The Kennedy Round was successful in producing a cut of 35 percent of manufactured goods, and less successful in reducing tariffs on agricultural products, only a 20 percent cut having been negotiated. Agricultural production has turned out to be a sore spot and the source of many retaliatory actions between the U.S. and the EEC as well as between the U.S. and Japan.

U.S. Trade Policy in the 1970s

Although free trade had been the self-described trade policy of past administrations, during the 1970s U.S. trade policy shifted from a free trade policy to one based on "reciprocity." The objective was to force other nations to give up practices which injured U.S. producers. Using this approach, if a nation failed to meet the reciprocity conditions, special restrictions and/or tariffs conceivably could be imposed on its exports to the United States. The origins of this change in policy can be traced to the passage of the Trade Act of 1974.

For the first time, the president was authorized to negotiate orderly marketing agreements as a form of relief under the escape clause. The act also required the fulfillment of reciprocity in trade concessions before a trade agreement between the U.S. and another major industrial country could be binding. In short, the Trade Act of 1974 permitted any industry, when threatened by imports, to seek and obtain protection.

THE U.S.-EEC TRADE POLICY

A summary of major trade action by the EEC is presented in Table 2.1. For additional information on unilateral trade actions by EEC member countries, see Table 2.2.

The EEC Trade Policies during the 1960s

During the 1960s, in addition to being engaged in the Kennedy Round negotiations, the European community was also involved in internal negotiation regarding its common market. A key feature of the common market plan was the lowering of internal tariffs among its member countries while making uniform barriers to trade from the outside. This as-

TABLE 2.1.   Summary of Major Trade Actions: EEC (1960–83)

Year	Free Trade Activities	Protectionist Activities
1961		Signed 16-nation pact to regulate trade in cotton textiles.
1962	Agreed with the U.S. to reduce tariffs on commodities representing $2 billion in annual trade. Tariffs reduced by 20 percent on wide range of industrial products and some agricultural products.	Raised tariffs on imports from U.S. on glass, carpet, and other man-made textiles: Polystyrene, Polyethylene (from 20 percent to 40 percent), synthetic cloth (from 17 percent to 40 percent), and varnishes and paints (from 15 percent to 19 percent). Increased tariffs on zinc and lead. Refused to reduce tariffs on poultry.
1966	Agreed with U.S. to reduce tariffs by as much as 50 percent on a wide range of goods: principally chemical products, machinery, precision instruments, and mass-produced consumer goods. (Some of the agreed reductions were contingent upon elimination of the American selling price.) Agreed to sign Kennedy Round Pact, reducing tariffs on goods amounting to $40 million in world trade.	
1967	Cut tariffs on U.S. exports of polystyrene and fabrics woven of synthetic fibers.	
1968	Proposed to speed up tariff cuts negotiated under the Kennedy Round.	Proposed to levy tariffs on soybean products from U.S. (U.S. threatened retaliation, since it would affect $500 million in trade.)
1969		Postponed scheduled tariff cuts on benzenoid chemical.
1970	Agreed with Japan to eliminate quota restrictions in trade over the following three years. Threatened the U.S. with reprisals if the U.S. passed a bill setting quotas on imports of textiles and shoes from EEC.	
1971	Cut tariff on U.S. oranges to 8 percent from 15 percent.	Agreed to subsidize producers of canned fruits and vegetables.

TABLE 2.1. *(continued)*

Year	Free Trade Activities	Protectionist Activities
1975		Reinstated subsidy of cheese products.
1976	Lifted ban on imports of beef from U.S.	Raised duty on turkey parts from the U.S. and imposed tax on soybean production.
1977		Imposed 20 percent countervailing duties on ball and tapered rolling bearings from Japan.
1978		Introduced licensing system for imports of shoes.
1979	Signed the Tokyo Round Pact.	
1980	Adopted (with U.S.) new method of valuing imports using transactions price (U.S. agreed to end American selling price).	
1981	Agreed to end internal restrictions on wine and poultry.	Imposed 14.8 percent antidumping duties on imports of styrene monomer and 38 percent duty on fabrics of texture polyester fibers from US. Signed the new Multifibre Agreement regulating trade in textiles.
1982		Imposed tax on U.S. cereal substitutes, corn gluten feed. Increased duties on imports of steel. Agreed to limit steel exports to the U.S. to 5.76 percent U.S. market.
1983		Announced plan to tax vegetable oils and animal fats.

pect of the common market plan resulted in some friction with the United States, which demanded lower tariff. However, the European Economic Community refused to make concessions, largely due to Charles de Gaulle's demand for farm policies that would make the EEC self-sufficient.

TABLE 2.2. Unilateral Trade Actions by EEC Member Countries

Year	Country	Action
1960	United Kingdom	Lifted curbs on imports from Canada of tobacco, tobacco products, and fish products.
1964	United Kingdom	Imposed 15 percent surcharge on imports of goods other than foodstuffs and industrial materials. Also cut export tax by 1.5 percent by value.
1965	United Kingdom	Reduced loan rates to exporters and instituted rebates ranging from 1 percent to $3^1/_4$ percent of value.
1966	United Kingdom	Eliminated import surcharge.
	Germany	Raised "border taxes" to 10 percent on imports.
1968	United Kingdom	Instituted cash deposit requirement on imports.
	France	Announced plans to place import quotas on automobiles, appliances, some textile and steel products.
1969	Germany	Imposed 5 percent import tax on farm products except poultry, eggs, fruit, and vegetables.
1972	United Kingdom	Reimposed 5 percent import tax on beef and veal after having suspended it for one month.
1973	United Kingdom	Became a member of the EEC along with Ireland and Denmark, joining the original six members.
1974	Italy	Imposed cash deposit requirement of 50 percent of value on imports.
1975	United Kingdom	Lifted bar on import of pork from U.S.
1980	United Kingdom	Restricted imports (by use of quotas) on polyester filament yarn, nylon carpet yarn, and tufted carpets of synthetic fibers from U.S. and Canada.
	France	Imposed requirement of "administrative visas" on importers of velvet, furs, and sponge cloth.

The U.S. Response to the EEC Trade Policies

In response to the EEC trade actions by the Common Market, the Kennedy-Johnson administration imposed retaliatory measures on the EEC. It is worthwhile to note that the nature of the U.S. response was well within the guidelines of GATT. The United States argued that the EEC actions that led within two years to a tripling of the tariff on poultry was depriving its domestic producers of $26 million of export trade.

Therefore, it argued that either the restriction by rescinded or that other trade compensation be offered.[1]

The United States retaliated by increasing tariffs on various EEC exports. Most affected was Volkswagen, which faced a tariff increase to 25 percent from 8.5 percent on small trucks, amounting to a $200 disadvantage per truck. The policy had no effect on imported automobiles. In response to these actions the EEC countered with an offer to trim its tariff on poultry by 10 percent.[2]

The EEC Response to U.S. Trade Policy

During the 1960s, the EEC responses to U.S. actions were also within the guidelines of GATT. For example, in response to the increase in U.S. trade restrictions on sheet glass and carpets, the EEC retaliated with an increase in tariffs on a variety of goods: polystyrene and polyethylene to 40 percent from 20 percent, synthetic cloth to 40 percent from 17 percent, and varnish and paints to 19 percent from 15 percent. These increases merely returned the tariffs to their old levels prior to the concessions made in previous negotiations.[3]

The protectionist mood was not unique to the United States. The EEC, in light of increasing cheese stocks, considered reinstating export subsidies on cheese products. The United States argued that such subsidies were in violation of U.S. countervailing duty law. Similarly, in response to a proposed tax on soybeans by the EEC, the United States warned that it would take retaliatory action by raising duties on an equivalent amount of EEC imports into the United States.[4]

The Reciprocal Trade Act

Not all of the actions between the United States and the EEC were of a retaliatory vein. During this time, under the then existing Reciprocal Trade Act, the United States and the EEC agreed to tariff reduction measures. The EEC slashed tariffs 20 percent on a whole range of imports from the United States (i.e., it affected $2 billion worth of trade). In turn, the United States reduced tariffs to then lower levels allowed under the trade act.

The EEC also made concessions on agricultural products. It agreed on a variable levy system where tariffs on agricultural imports were based on the difference between home and foreign prices. Unfortunately, at the same time, the EEC established an agricultural fund for supporting prices, paying export subsidies in hopes of easing the transition to a free agricultural market in the EEC. This result is yet to be accomplished.

With some exceptions, the move toward less restrictions on manufactured goods continued throughout the decade. The EEC's finance ministers agreed to speed up the Kennedy Round tariff cuts in return for the United States abolishing its "American selling price."[5] The French, however, were reluctant to make concessions.[6]

Notice that the movement toward more open free trade was not an unequivocal endorsement of free trade. Rather, the action of the United States and its major trading partners suggests a policy of balancing the goal of free trade with a desire to equalize harm. Obviously, one special case of this policy is that of "zero harm," i.e., "free trade."

U.S.-JAPAN TRADE POLICY

With the emergence of the Japanese economy in the 1960s, U.S. and EEC efforts were increasingly directed to Japan. A summary of major trade actions by Japan is reported in Table 2.3.

The Nature of Japan Trade Policy

Upon inspection of Table 2.3, it is apparent that throughout this period Japan had followed a fairly protectionist policy on a variety of products. It allowed imports of only the most expensive, top-of-the-line models. In response to U.S. pressure, Japan in 1961 unilaterally reduced tariff and nontariff barriers on 20 items. However, the United States indicated that while progress was being made, further negotiation was required. These apparent unilateral concessions to the United States were clearly in response to the threat of potential retaliatory actions by the United States. The emergence of Japan as an economic power and its dependency on international trade forced Japan to comply with GATT in addition to making concessions to the United States. The strategy followed by Japan throughout this period appears to have been to comply with GATT in the line of products in which Japan gained comparative advantage.

U.S.-Japan Trade Policy in the 1970s

During the 1970s as U.S. trade policy shifted from free trade to "fair" trade, the use of "voluntary export restraints" also expanded. Un-

TABLE 2.3. Summary of Major Trade Actions: Japan (1960–83)

Year	Free Trade Activities	Protectionist Activities
1960	Lifted import curbs on 257 items, including pig iron, machinery, chemical and rubber goods, materials, and mineral products.	Voluntarily placed quotas on exports of transistor radios to U.S.
1961	Reduced tariffs and nontariff barriers on 20 items, including raisins, bourbon, machine tools, musical instruments, and fountain pens.	Signed 16-nation pact restricting imports of cotton textiles.
1962		Raised tariff barriers on a variety of items, including outboard motors, industrial lathes, drill presses, and milling machines.
1967	Signed the Kennedy Round pact covering over 1,000 industrial and agricultural products, with many of the reductions on industrial machinery, etc., amounting to 50 percent.	
1968	Eased import quotas on auto parts and engines from 1,000 to 30,000 units.	Offered voluntarily to curb steel exports to U.S. with a ceiling of 5 million tons a year.
1970	Reduced foreign auto tariffs by 10 percentage points. Agreed with EEC progressively to abolish 75 percent of all quota restrictions over the following three years. Eliminated quotas on imports on some commodities, including dried coffee, flour, fruits, roes of cod and herring, gluten, some drugs, and some industrial machinery.	
1971	Removed quotas on a variety of agricultural products and communication equipment. 26 categories taken off the Automatic Quota Schedule. (Tariffs on many items freed of quota restrictions were raised: see Protectionist Activities)	Agreed to limit exports of textile products and stainless flatware. Raised tariffs on live cattle and pigs, fishmeal, raw oils for menthol, and dextrine.
1972	Dropped nine-year old "Buy Japan"	

TABLE 2.3. *(continued)*

Year	Free Trade Activities	Protectionist Activities
	rule that required all government-supported activities to buy at home.	
	Reduced tariffs by 10 percent on soybean oil, computers and computer equipment, machine tools, and color and X-ray films.	
1973	Allowed export controls on 20 items to expire.	
1977	Lifted ban on imports of lemon and grapefruit from U.S.	
1978	Agreed to tariffs reduced on 300 items and removal of quotas on 11 agricultural products affecting $2 billion of imports from U.S. Major items affected were beef, oranges, and citrus juice.	Agreed to limit textile and apparel exports to U.S. at the 1977 levels. Agreed to limit steel exports to EEC. Agreed voluntarily to limit auto exports to the United Kingdom.
1979	Agreed to remove restrictions on leather imports from U.S. Signed the Tokyo Round Pact negotiated under GATT.	
1980	Agreed to ease restrictions on imports of U.S.-made cigarettes and tobacco products.	
1981		Signed the Multifibre Agreement controlling world trade in cotton wool and synthetic textiles.
1982	Introduced package of reforms to eliminate nontariff barriers such as customs procedures and produce testing.	
1983	Agreed to eliminate tariffs on semiconductors.	Extended voluntary curbs on auto exports to U.S. and video tape recorders to EEC.

der this arrangement, the importing country negotiates an agreement with the exporting country to limit ''voluntarily'' the amounts of certain exports. In the United States, such negotiated trade restrictions, in the form of orderly marketing agreements, have been imposed on specialty steels, color TV receivers, nonrubber footwear, certain meats, mushrooms, textiles, and automobiles. In 1976 the president obtained an orderly marketing agreement to limit specialty steel exports with Japan, and unilateral quotas were imposed on imports from the EEC and other countries. While the United States negotiated these orderly marketing agreements with Japan, the EEC warned that it may have to retaliate to safeguard its rights with reprisals against Japan, and against the United States if the U.S. limited imports from the EEC. Under GATT the ECC was clearly within its rights to impose countermeasures.[7]

During this period, Japan continued to yield to U.S. pressures by reducing some trade barriers on U.S. agricultural products by either eliminating nontariff agreement, such as potential health hazards, or lifting the embargo on U.S.-produced lemons and grapefruit treated with 0-ophenylphenol fungicide. Other forms of reduction of trade barriers included bilateral trade negotiations.[8]

OTHER DEVELOPMENTS

The Trade Act of 1979 overhauled the U.S. countervailing laws designed to protect domestic industries against foreign government subsidies on imported goods. In particular, the act facilitated and resulted in a speeding up of the investigation and imposition of penalties under countervailing duty and antidumping laws. It also established new custom valuations which used the prices actually paid for merchandise when sold for exportation to the United States.

The move toward protectionism got another push when the domestic steel industry on January 11, 1982, filed forms with the Commerce Department and the International Trade Commission charging nine European countries, Brazil, and South Africa with unfair trade practices. On October 21, just hours before the Commerce Department would have been required to impose countervailing and penalty duties—selective increases in U.S. tariffs and duties—quota negotiations were finalized limiting European steel imports to about 85 percent of 1981 levels.

Administration arguments that the new trade restrictions were designed to foster the goals of the Williamsburg summit, by pressuring other nations to get rid of practices injuring U.S. producers, were fatuous. The European response was to threaten to retaliate with higher tariffs on U.S. exports to the Common Market. Furthermore, the U.S. actions ignored recent European moves reducing "unfair" trade practices. Prior to the economic summit, the Common Market countries had agreed to phase out the steel subsidies that were so offensive to U.S. producers and the administration. Yet, the higher tariffs and quotas were to prevail for four years.

This incident provides another explicit example of foreign countries' retaliating against the United States for its imposition of protectionist measures. In January of the following year, the EEC imposed new restrictions on U.S. exports of chemicals, sporting goods, and burglar alarms. The reason was to equalize the harm created by the U.S. quotas on European specialty steel.

NOTES

1. For a detailed explanation, see the following *Wall Street Journal* articles: "Refusal of the Common Market To Cut Tariffs on U.S. Poultry May Prompt Retaliation," as well as "Common Market May Offer 10 Percent Tariff Cut on Chickens To Get U.S. To Soften Boosts."

2. See *The Wall Street Journal,* "Common Market Raises Tariffs in Some U.S. Goods Effective Today."

3. On this issue, see Vicker (1962).

4. See *The Wall Street Journal* articles: "EEC To Reinstate Cheese-Export Subsidies and U.S. Gears Up for Battle Once More," and "European Soybean Tax Could Widely Damage Relations, U.S. Warns."

5. The American selling price applies tariffs to imported chemicals on the basis of prices in the United States rather than on their export values. For further detail on the measures taken, see Mellvan (1968).

6. See *The Wall Street Journal* article, "Benzenoid Chemical Tariff Cuts Postponed."

7. See *The Wall Street Journal* article, "EEC Warns of Reprisals."

8. Numerous articles on these issues appeared in *The Wall Street Journal.*

3

Sectoral Benefits and Costs of U.S. Trade Restrictions

ANALYTICAL FOUNDATION

The analytical foundation of this chapter is the observation that people respond to incentives. This simple but powerful observation and its implications for economic behavior are the basis for the classical tradition in economics. As part of that tradition, this analysis relates changes in trade policies to changes in incentives to engage in different market activities and to change in an economy's overall performance. Other things being equal, individuals allocate resources according to after-tax yields. If market activities are profitable, the economy will shun leisure and other nonmarket ventures while concentrating on ever-increasing market successes.[1] If, however, successful market performance encounters increasing discrimination in the form of high and progressive taxes, regulations, trade restrictions, and other forms of societal discouragement, economic activity will not achieve its potential.

The analysis also is based on the presumption that markets can be characterized as being efficient; that is, individual market participants incorporate available information concerning the present and future into current behavior. For example, if known, a restriction in trade for the next period will elicit some economic adjustment in the current period. In short, economic agents behave "rationally." That is, consumers maximize their well-being and producers maximize profits.

An embargo on the import or export of a specific commodity represents the extreme restriction on the trade of the given commodity across national boundaries. As will become apparent later on, the assump-

35

tion of an embargo will greatly simplify the presentation. The reason being that it is exactly equal to a quota set equal to zero on the export of the embargoed commodity. Under some general conditions, a quota, and thus an embargo, can be shown to be equivalent to a trade tax.[2] The analysis of the effects of an embargo may be used to explore the effects of trade restrictions—whether they are tariffs or quotas—in general.

There is a fairly extensive literature on theoretical models exploring the relationships among the initial and final incidence of a tax. The first of these papers is Arnold Harberger's (1962) classic paper. In the context of a closed economy, Harberger's theoretical work has been extended to analyze the sensitivity of industrial location to state tax and subsidy policies by McLure (1970). In his analysis, McLure examines the impact on capital flows of taxes on production, capital, and labor. McLure's analysis shows how the capital flows vary given different elasticities of product and factor demand and different factor mobility and factor substitution.

As long as the equivalence between quotas and tariffs holds, the effects of an embargo (a quota where exports or imports are set to zero) can be interpreted as a special case of a tax-incidence analysis. Choosing the proper scope of an incidence analysis is difficult. At one extreme is the traditional, partial equilibrium analysis. Such an analysis is often an important initial step but seldom an acceptable final one. At the other extreme is general equilibrium analysis. Such an approach incorporates every conceivable effect of the embargo in the many equations of the models of the analyzed economies. Consequently, the significance of the results, given their reliability, is almost impossible to determine. Somewhere between these two extremes lies the ideal, an approach that is manageable, yet neglects nothing of major importance. In our opinion, variants of the Harberger model represent the proper scope.[3]

THE ANALYSIS

Arbitrage insures relative price equalization across countries for any pair of tradable commodities. Economic agents buy products as cheaply as possible (lowest-priced locality) and sell in the highest-priced locality. Absent transportation costs, the dollar price of any commodity will be the same anywhere in the world. That is, absolute purchasing power parity will result.

The logic applies to factors of production as well as to commodities. Migration assures that factor prices will be equalized across countries.

If wage rates are higher in one country than another, workers will move or "vote with their feet." In the process, the supply of labor will increase in the higher-wage country, reducing wages there. This migration, in turn, will reduce the supply of labor in the rest of the world and raise the rest of the world's wage rate. Migration will continue until factor payments are equalized in all localities.[4] The same analysis applies to capital. If rates of return are higher in one country, capital will flow to that country until investment opportunities with above-average rates of return relative to the rest of the world are exhausted.

Initially, factors of production are assumed to be perfectly mobile across countries as is technology. Commodities also are assumed to be costlessly mobile. All countries have equal advantages in producing any commodity. Alternatively stated, no country will have a comparative advantage in any commodity being produced. Thus, if any country introduces a production tax on any commodity, that country will not produce the newly taxed commodity and 100 percent will be imported. Similarly, any country's tax on a consumption good will result in the total migration of all factors of production which consume the taxed product.

If the real world corresponded to such a frictionless world, any tax would completely exhaust the taxed activity in the locality where the tax was introduced, and both production and consumption would be absorbed by the rest of the world. World production and consumption would remain unchanged, and the location of production in specific, nontaxed countries would be a matter of indifference.

As a result, production, consumption, and employment in nontaxed areas cannot be determined without considering frictions. Once frictions are introduced, production, consumption, and expenditure patterns can be determined.

The analysis contained in this chapter focuses, in particular, on three frictions:

1. technological differences among countries;
2. the degree of factor mobility among countries;
3. the degree of factor mobility within national boundaries.

As these restrictions are introduced, more realistic implications of the incidence of a commodity embargo is developed.

The following section introduces technological differences across countries while assuming perfect factor mobility. For illustration purposes, only two countries, the United States and the rest of the world, are assumed. In the next section, a further complication is introduced: In addition to technological differences, factors of production are assumed to be immobile across national boundaries, but they remain perfectly mobile within their respective countries. This complication requires the introduction of a third country. Finally, the last section modifies the analysis of the previous section by adding restrictions on the mobility of capital across industries within a single country. Again, a three-country analysis is used.

Even with these restrictions, arbitrage insures relative price equalization across countries for any pair of tradable commodities. Economic agents buy products at the lowest-priced locality and sell them at the highest-priced locality. In the absence of transportation costs, the dollar price of any commodity will be the same anywhere in the world. That is, absolute purchasing power parity will result.

SCENARIO I:
A WORLD WITH PERFECT FACTOR MOBILITY
AND NONSUBSTITUTABLE GOODS

In a world of perfect factor mobility and unique goods, the initial effect of an embargo of a commodity imported into the United States is to increase the supply of the embargoed commodity in the rest of the world and to reduce the supply of the commodity in the United States. These shifts in supply imply a reduction in the rate of return to production of the embargoed commodity in the rest of the world and an increase in the rate of return in the United States.

Since the United States does not have the technology to produce the embargoed commodity (i.e., by assumption, the embargoed commodity has no domestic substitute), domestic producers will not be able to benefit from the high rate of return in producing the embargoed commodity. The rest of the world, on the other hand, must absorb the factors of production released by the decrease in production of the embargoed commodity. This tends to alter the rest of the world rates of return vis-à-vis the United States.

Such an environment invites migration of both labor and capital. If factors previously employed to produce the embargoed commodity migrate from the rest of the world to the United States (i.e., foreign firms relocate in the United States), world prices, output, and consumption need not change.[5] However, both countries' international and national income accounts will change. The rest of the country's GNP will decline, exports will decrease and capital inflow (i.e., repatriation of capital) will increase. That is, the merchandise trade balance in the rest of the world will deteriorate, while the capital account will improve. The sum of the two, GNP, will remain unchanged.

For the United States, the opposite results will occur. Thus, no significant change in GNP and the goods and services trade balance will take place. In short, the embargo will have no fundamental impact on either country.

SCENARIO II: A WORLD WITH FACTOR MOBILITY ONLY WITHIN NATIONAL BOUNDARIES

In the case where factors may not move across national boundaries, an embargo may still be fully offset by changes in production patterns and trade. In this case, two factors of production which are freely mobile within a country but immobile across national boundaries are assumed. Three commodities are produced in this world, and some of the countries are assumed to have inferior technology in the production of one or another of the three commodities.[6]

There are a total of three countries. One country, East, has an efficient technology in all three commodities. The second, the United States, has an inferior technology in the production of the third commodity (C). The third country, the rest of the world, has an inferior technology in the second commodity (B). Finally, it is assumed that the three countries always engage in free trade in at least two commodities. This assumption assures that factor prices are equalized across countries.

If the United States embargoes the importation of a commodity in which it has inferior technology, say commodity C, from East, the only effect the embargo will have is to alter the patterns of trade among countries without affecting world consumption, production, or prices. The general standard of living also will be unaffected. The embargo will be ineffective.[7]

Intuitively, if the United States prohibits the importing of commodity C from East, East's production of commodity C will decline. Factors previously used to produce commodity C can now produce the other two commodities, B and A. The rest of the world, which has technology equivalent to that in East in the production of commodity C, will increase its output, thereby absorbing factors from the production of commodity A. The rest of the world will produce more of commodity C and less of commodity A. Thus, it will export more of commodity C and import more of commodity A. The United States, on the other hand, will import commodity C from the rest of the world instead of from East.

Because factors are mobile within countries and at least one other country has technology equivalent to that in the United States, world prices and world consumption will not be altered by the U.S. import embargo. Each country's well-being will remain the same. Production patterns and the patterns of trade, however, will change.

In this example, the rest of the world literally offsets the U.S. embargo on imports from East. For the restrictions on imports to be effective, the import embargo must also apply to the rest of the world.

Even a universal restriction on the import of commodity C, however, is not sufficient to guarantee that the embargo will reduce output in any of the three countries; the choice of the commodity embargoed also matters. An import prohibition on one of the commodities in which the United States has an efficient technology means that the United States need only reduce the production and increase the imports of nonembargoed commodities and increase the domestic production of the embargoed commodity. Since trade occurs in two other commodities, factor prices will remain equalized.

Even in the case where the United States has an inferior technology, if the embargo is permanent, then it may benefit the United States to acquire efficient technology to produce the commodity in question. To summarize:

1. If the U.S. import restriction is to be successful in protecting its industry, the embargo must apply to all countries that possess the technology to produce the embargoed commodity.
2. The overall economic effect of a quota depends a great deal on the choice of the commodity restricted. If the United States chooses a commodity for which it has an equivalent technology, the embargo will not reduce the level of overall output or employment, just the distribution of employment and output.
3. A quota will reduce the standard of living in the United States to the extent that it reduces the consumption levels of the embargoed commodity. The economic cost to the United States will be both inversely related to the efficiency level of U.S. technology used in the production of the embargoed commodity and indirectly related to the share of the U.S. income (i.e., expenditures) devoted to the purchase (production) of the embargoed commodity.
4. The embargo will increase production levels in the protected industry if the technology used to manufacture the commodity can be imported.

5. Even if the embargo applies to the import of a commodity for which the United States has an inferior technology and it is not possible to import the technology (summary points 2, 3, and 4), the economic cost of the embargo will diminish over time as the United States develops efficient technology.

Obviously, if the technology is easily acquired so that all countries are equally efficient, a quota may be imposed. If, on the other hand, new technology is not available, it will increase the rate of return on new investment in the areas. Clearly, over time, as the new technology is developed, new investment takes place and the domestic industry expands; the "excess" returns from investing in these areas will decline toward a normal rate of return.

SCENARIO III: A WORLD IN WHICH THE CAPITAL OF EACH INDUSTRY IS IN PLACE (I.E., IMMOBILE ACROSS INDUSTRIES AND/OR COUNTRIES)

This section assumes that the import restrictions are totally effective. Furthermore, labor is assumed to be completely mobile across industries while capital is immobile.[8]

A U.S. embargo on the importation of commodity C will remove domestic demand for the embargoed commodity. Consequently, there will be a decline in the foreign price of the embargoed commodity as well as a decline in the rate of return on the capital employed to produce commodity C in country East and the rest of the world. At the same time, the price of commodity C will rise in the United States, as will the wages paid and the rate of return for labor and capital, respectively, used in the production of the embargoed commodity.

As a result, the import embargo will alter sector-specific investment patterns. The U.S. industry's incentive would be to invest more in the embargoed sector, while for country East and the rest of the world, the opposite would be true.

An investment occurs in the activities with the highest returns, the rate of return to capital in each sector will again be equalized. Trade in the remaining two commodities assures factor price equalization.

In the short run, the capital stock is in place and cannot be moved to other sectors of the economy. As a result, the embargo will entail some adjustment costs. The short-run effects on the United States and its trading partners economies' well-being are more complicated than in the case where capital is mobile across industries. But, in any case, output, employment, and the general standard of living are diminished in the United States as well as in its trading partners. How much each country will be hurt depends upon the distribution of capital among the different industries in each country and the fixity of the capital in each country.

If the capital in place in each industry is close to the capital stock required to satisfy the domestic consumption (i.e., the economy is closer to its autarky levels), then the impact of the embargo will be minimal.[9] Similarly, the larger the level of trade between the various countries, the larger the difference between the capital stock in place in the various industries and the amount required to satisfy the level of domestic consumption. Thus, given that the capital is in place, then the imposition of an embargo will generate the largest change in the derived demand for the capital in various industries. The larger the level of trade, therefore, the larger the impact on the rate of return on these factors.

In the longer run, as capital depreciates and new investment takes place, the stock of capital in any one industry or country will no longer be fixed. Alternatively stated, in the long run, the effect of an embargo will be to alter the patterns of trade and production (no trade in the embargoed commodity). However, the level of worldwide production and individual country's consumption will move back to where it would have been, absent the embargo.

The amount of capital employed in the embargoed industries will be precisely sufficient and yield the same return as does capital employed in other sectors. In an embargoed product's industry, capital will be just sufficient to meet domestic demands.

In the final analysis, the best result is that an embargo has no net effect on output or employment in the United States. However, even in this best case, the adjustment costs implied by the position of a quota mean that the U.S. economy as a whole is poorer as the result of an embargo.

Notice that, in principle, the embargo could also be used to provide "breathing room" to certain domestic industries which, for some reason, have failed to introduce efficient technology. The danger in doing this is that, once these protective policies are implemented, the protected industries have no incentive to introduce the new technology until their existing (inefficient) capital is totally consumed. Thus, one courts the danger of having to continually protect inefficient industries.

In the final analysis, the last result shown in this section is that an embargo has no net effect on output and employment in the United States. However, the analysis shows that, as frictions are introduced, the embargo may have real effects on the U.S. economy. These may be fairly large in the short run when the economy has no possibility of adjusting to the government action and will tend to disappear over the longer run as the economy is able to alter the technologies, capital stock production, and employment levels of the various industries.

Our analysis is based on efficiency arguments. While we can show that in the absence of monopoly power (in which case a producer could improve its well-being by exercising such monopoly power, e.g., OPEC), the efficiency of the economy declines. As a result, there will be resources involved with various measures. This does not imply that all sectors of the economy lose from these actions. There may be, in fact, groups who benefit (i.e., the argument for protective policy to provide "breathing room" that will increase the return to capital above what it would otherwise be in the unprotected industries). This suggests that if, in addition to the efficiency effect, the distributional impact of the various actions are taken into consideration and different groups are given different weights, it may be possible to argue that these protective policies are desirable.

NOTES

1. For a detailed treatment of the effects of tax rates on economic activities see Canto, Joines, and Laffer (1983).

2. For a discussion of the precise conditions under which the equivalence holds, see Chapter 5, Laffer and Miles (1981).

3. On the issue see Break (1974).

4. Perfect factor mobility is a sufficient but not a necessary condition for the equalization of factor prices across countries. Under some general conditions, trade in goods may be sufficient to equalize factor prices. See Samuelson (1948, 1949). The effects of factor migrations in the equation of prices are also well known. See Mundell (1957) and Samuelson (1965).

5. To a large extent, this has been the experience in the U.S. color television market. See V. A. Canto and A.B. Laffer (1983). Orderly marketing agreements for color television, negotiated by the U.S. government and beginning in 1977, function as import quotas. They have encouraged Japanese producers to locate plants in the United States. In effect, the weaker U.S. firms that were driven from the market by import competition have been replaced by foreign firms manufacturing in the United States. The Japanese are being followed by companies based in Taiwan and Korea.

6. With free trade, inferior technologies will not be used. Thus a country with inferior technology will import all it consumes of that commodity.

7. A formal derivation of the results stated in this section can be found in Appendix B.

8. A formal derivation of the results stated in this section can be found in Appendix C.

9. This is almost a truism for, if the country is close to its autarky level, we are implicitly saying that there are no gains from trade. Therefore, there should be no losses due to the prohibition of trade.

APPENDIX A: SOLUTION TO THE WORLDWIDE EQUILIBRIUM PRICES AND OUTPUT LEVELS ABSENT TRADE RESTRICTIONS

Worldwide Equilibrium

Assumptions

1. There are two factors of production: capital (K) and labor (L).
2. Factors are assumed to be mobile within countries but not across national boundaries.
3. The technology is assumed to be Cobb-Douglas.
4. Preferences are assumed to be Cobb-Douglas.
5. Producers are assumed to maximize profits.
6. Consumers are assumed to maximize utility.
7. Two commodities are assumed to be produced in this world economy.
8. Perfect competition.

The Technology

$$(1) \qquad Q_i^W = (b_i K_i^W)^{b_i}[(1-b_i)L_i^W]^{(1-b_i)}$$

where Q_i^W denotes the world production of the ith commodity, K_i^W and L_i^W the amount of world physical units of capital employed in the production of the ith commodity, b_i and $(1-b_i)$ the partial output elasticities of capital and labor. The Cobb-Douglas technology and profit maximizations yield the following Cobb-Douglas cost functions.

$$(2) \qquad P_i = R^{b_i} W^{(1-b_i)}$$

where P_i denotes the average and marginal cost of producing the ith commodity. R and W the marginal product of capital and labor respectively. A property of a Cobb-Douglas function is the constancy of factor shares. That is:

$$(3) \qquad b_i = \frac{R(b_i K_i^W)}{P_i Q_i^W}$$

$$(4) \qquad (1-b_i) = \frac{W(1-b_i)L_i^W}{P_i Q_i^W}$$

Preferences

$$(5) \qquad U^W = C_1^{q_1} C_2^{q_2}$$

where U^W denotes the world preference function, C_i world consumption of ith commodity, and a_i the partial output elasticity of the preference function. Notice that $a_1 + a_2 = 1$. The Cobb-Douglas preference function yields a constant share of income being spent on each commodity. Thus:

(6) $\qquad a_i = \dfrac{P_i C_i^W}{I^W}$

where I^W denotes the world income. Utility maximizations yield the cost of living index (i.e., the numeraire).

(7) $\qquad 1 = P_a^{a_1} P_2^{a_2}$

Solution to the Equilibrium Values of the Factor Rewards

The worldwide employment of labor can be expressed as:

$$L^W = L_1^W + L_2^W$$

Substituting equation 6 into equation 4 and then into the previous equation yields

(8) $\qquad L^W = S_L \left(\dfrac{I^W}{W} \right)$

where

(9) $\qquad S_L = (1 - b_1)a_1 + (1 - b_2)a_2$

is defined as labor share of world income. Similarly,

(10) $\qquad K^W = S_K \left(\dfrac{I^W}{R} \right)$

(11) $\qquad S_K = b_1 a_1 + b_2 a_2$

Notice that:

(12) $\qquad 1 = S_L + S_K$

Dividing equation 10 by equation 8 yields an expression for the world-wide wage-rental rate (W/R).

(13) $\quad \dfrac{W}{R} = \left(\dfrac{K^W}{L^W} \, \dfrac{S_L}{S_K} \right)$

Substituting equations 13 into the numeraire (equation 7) yields:

(14) $\quad W = \left(\dfrac{W}{R} \right)^{S_K} = \left(\dfrac{K^W}{L^W} \, \dfrac{S_L}{S_K} \right)^{S_K}$

From equations 13 and 14 one can solve for the rental rate.

(15) $\quad R = W \left(\dfrac{R}{W} \right) = \left(\dfrac{K^W}{L^W} \, \dfrac{S_L}{S_K} \right)^{-S_L}$

Product Prices

Substituting equations 14 and 15 into 2 yields:

(16) $\quad P_i = \left(\dfrac{K^W}{L^W} \, \dfrac{S_L}{S_K} \right)^{S_K - b_i}$

World Income

$$I^W = R K^W + W L^W = \left[\dfrac{R K^W}{W L^W} + 1 \right] W L^W = \dfrac{W L^W}{S_L}$$

Substituting equation 14 into the previous equation:

(17) $\quad I^W = \left(\dfrac{K^W}{S_K} \right)^{S_K} \left(\dfrac{L^W}{S_L} \right)^{S_L}$

World Sectoral Output

The world is a closed economy, thus in equilibrium. World production will equal world consumption. Thus, from equation 6, one obtains an expression for world consumption.

$$Q_i^W = C_i^W = a_i \, \dfrac{I^W}{P_i}$$

Substituting equations 16 and 17 into the previous equations one obtains

$$(18) \qquad Q_i^W = C_i^W = a_i \left(\frac{K^W}{S_K} \right)^{b_i} \left(\frac{L^W}{S_L} \right)^{b_i - (S_L - S_K)}$$

Sectoral Employment

Substituting equations 16 and 18 into equations 3 and 4 yields the sectoral employment

$$(19) \qquad L_i^W = \frac{P_i Q_i}{W} = a_i \left(\frac{L^W}{S_L} \right)$$

$$(20) \qquad K_i^W = \frac{P_i Q_i}{R_i} = a_i \left(\frac{K^W}{S_K} \right)$$

Individual Country's Consumption, Production, and Patterns of Trade

Assumptions

1. There are two countries in this world economy. They are: the U.S. and the East.
2. For all commodities, both countries are assumed to have the same technology (i.e., as in equation 1).
3. Trade is assumed to be balanced (i.e., the value of imports equals the value of exports).
4. There are no transportation costs.
5. The countries are assumed to have different factor endowment.

Implications of the Assumptions

1. Since each country has at least two traded commodities, factor price equalizations will obtain.
2. The assumptions of exogenous factors endowment combined with the free trade assumptions imply that world production and consumption levels, as well as factor rewards, are the same as in Worldwide Equilibrium section above.

Income of Individual Countries

The countries differ only by the scale of their factor endowments. Thus:

$$(21) \qquad I^{US} = S_{US} \, I^W$$

(22) $I^E = S_F \, I^W$

(23) $I^R = S_R \, I^W$

where S_i denotes the ith country share of world resources.

Individual Countries' Consumption of the Different Commodities

(24) $C_i^1 = S_1 \, Q_1 = S_1 a_i \left(\dfrac{K^W}{S_K} \right)^{b_i} \left(\dfrac{L^W}{S_L} \right)^{b_i(S_L - S_K)}$

where index 1 denotes the country and i the commodity.

U.S. and East Sectoral Employment

The economy's factor employment equation can be expressed as:

$$\frac{K^1}{L^1} = \frac{L_1^1}{L^1} \left(\frac{b_1 K_1}{(1-b_1)L_1} \right) + \left(1 - \frac{L_1^1}{L} \right) \left(\frac{b_1 K_2}{(1-b_2)\, L_2} \right)$$

Substituting equations 3 and 4 into

$$\frac{b_2 K_2}{(1-b_2)\, L_2}$$

and noting that

$$\frac{K^W}{L^W} = \frac{K^1}{L^i}$$

one can derive an expression for the sectoral demand for effective units of labor. Thus, the U.S. Sectoral Employment of Labor Services can be expressed as:

(25) $L_1^{US} = L^{US} \left[\dfrac{(1-b_2)\,(K^{US}/K^W)\,(L^W/L^{US})\,(S_K/S_L) - b_1\,(1-b_1)}{(b_1 - b_2)} \right]$

(26) $L_1^{US} = L^{US} \left[\dfrac{b_2(1-b_2) - (K^{US}/K^W)\,(L^W/L^{US})\,(S^K/S^L)\,(1-b_1)}{(b_1 - b_2)} \right]$

Sectoral Employment of Capital Services

(27) $\quad K_1^{US} = \left(\dfrac{K^W}{L^W} \ \dfrac{S_L}{S_K} \right) L_2^{US}$

(28) $\quad K_2^{US} = \left(\dfrac{K^W}{L^W} \ \dfrac{S_L}{S_K} \right) L_2^{US}$

Sectoral Output

(29) $\quad Q_1^{US} = b_1^{b_1}(1-b_1)^{\ (1-b_1)} L^{US} \left(\dfrac{K^W}{L^W} \ \dfrac{S_L}{S_K} \right)^{b_1}$

$$\left[\dfrac{\left(1-b_2\right) (K^{US}/K^W) (L^W/L^{US}) (S_K/S_L) - b_1 \ (1-b_1)}{b_1 - b_2} \right]$$

(30) $\quad Q_2^{US} = b_2^{b_2}(1-b_2)^{(1-b_2)} \ L^{US} \left(\dfrac{K^W}{L^W} \ \dfrac{S_L}{S_K} \right)^{b_2}$

$$\left[\dfrac{b_2(1-b_2) - (K^{US}/K^W) \ (L^W/L^{US}) \ (S_K/S_L) \ (1-b_1)}{b_1 - b_2} \right]$$

The U.S. net trade position is derived from the consumption and production equation as follows: $M_1^{US} = C_1^{US} - Q_1^{US}$. East's sectoral output by employment and net trade position are obtained by substituting the superscript in place of *US*. Finally, the autarky solution for each country is obtained by substituting the country superscript in place of the world superscript.

APPENDIX B: SOLUTION TO THE EFFECTS OF AN EMBARGO ON THE WORLDWIDE EQUILIBRIUM PRICES, OUTPUT, AND PATTERNS OF TRADE

Worldwide Equilibrium

Assumptions

1. There are two factors of production: capital (K) and labor (L).

2. Factors are assumed to be mobile within countries but not across national boundaries.
3. The technology is assumed to be Cobb-Douglas.
4. Preferences are assumed to be Cobb-Douglas.
5. Producers are assumed to maximize profits.
6. Consumers are assumed to maximize utility.
7. Three commodities are assumed to be produced in this world economy.
8. Perfect competition.

The Technology

(1) $Q_i^W = (b_i K_i^W)^{b_i} (1-b_i)L_i^{W \ (1-b_i)}$

where Q_i^W denotes the world production of the *i*th commodity; K_i^W and L_i^W the amount of world physical units of capital employed in the production of the *i*th commodity; b_i and $(1-b_i)$ the partial output elasticities of capital and labor. The Cobb-Douglas technology and profit maximizations yield the following Cobb-Douglas cost functions.

(2) $P_i = R^{b_i} W^{(1-b_i)}$

where P_i denotes the average and marginal cost of producing the *i*th commodity, and R and W the marginal product of capital and labor respectively. A property of a Cobb-Douglas function is the constancy of factor shares. That is:

(3) $b_i = \dfrac{R(b_i K_i^W)}{P_i Q_i^W}$

(4) $(1-b_i) = \dfrac{W\,(1-b_i)L_i^W}{P_i Q_i^W}$

Preferences

(5) $U^W = C_1^{a_1}\, C_2^{a_2}\, C_3^{a_3}$

where U^W denotes the world preference function, C_i world consumption of *i*th commodity, and a_i the partial output elasticity of the preference function. Notice that $a_1 + a_2 + a_3 = 1$. The Cobb-Douglas preference function yields a constant share of income being spent on each commodity. Thus:

$$(6) \qquad a_i = \frac{P_i C_i^W}{I^W}$$

where I^W denotes the world income.

Utility maximizations yield the cost of living index (i.e., the numeraire).

$$(7) \qquad 1 = P_a^{a_1} P_2^{q_2} P_3^{q_3}$$

Solution to the Equilibrium Values of the Factor Rewards

The worldwide employment of labor can be expressed as:

$$L^W = L_1^W + L_2^W + L_3^W$$

Substituting equation 6 into equation 4 and then into the previous equation yields

$$(8) \qquad L^W = S_L \left(\frac{I^W}{W} \right)$$

where

$$(9) \qquad S_L = (1-b_1)a_1 + (1-b_2)a_2 + (1-b_3)a_3$$

is defined as labor share of world income. Similarly,

$$(10) \qquad K^W = S_K \left(\frac{I^W}{R} \right)$$

$$(11) \qquad S_K = b_1 a_1 + b_2 a_2 + b_3 a_3$$

Notice that:

$$(12) \qquad 1 = S_L + S_K$$

Dividing equation 10 by equation 8 yields an expression for the worldwide wage-rental rate (W/R).

$$(13) \quad \frac{W}{R} = \left(\frac{K^W}{L^W} \frac{S_L}{S_K} \right)$$

Substituting equation 13 into the numeraire (equation 7) yields:

$$(14) \quad W = \left(\frac{W}{R} \right)^{S_K} = \left(\frac{K^W}{L^W} \frac{S_L}{S_K} \right)^{S_K}$$

From equations 13 and 14 one can solve for the rental rate.

$$(15) \quad R = W\left(\frac{R}{W} \right) = \left(\frac{K^W}{L^W} \frac{S_L}{S_K} \right)^{-S_L}$$

Product Prices

Substituting equations 14 and 15 into 2 yields:

$$(16) \quad P_i = \left(\frac{K^W}{L^W} \frac{S_L}{S_K} \right)^{S_K - b_i}$$

World Income

$$I^W = RK^W + WL^W = \left[\frac{RK^W}{WL^W} + 1 \right] WL^W = \frac{WL^W}{S_L}$$

Substituting equation 14 into the previous equation:

$$(17) \quad I^W = \left(\frac{K^W}{S_K} \right)^{S_K} \left(\frac{L^W}{S_L} \right)^{S_L}$$

World Sectoral Output

The world is a closed economy, thus in equilibrium. World production will equal world consumption. Thus, from equation 6, one obtains an expression for world consumption.

$$Q_i^W = C_i^W = a_i \frac{I^W}{P_i}$$

Substituting equations 16 and 17 into the previous equation one obtains:

$$(18) \qquad Q_i^W = C_i^W = a_i \left(\frac{K^W}{SK} \right)^{b_i} \left(\frac{L^W}{SL} \right)^{b_i - (SL - SK)}$$

Sectoral Employment

Substituting equations 16 and 18 yields the sectoral employment:

$$(19) \qquad L_i^W = \frac{P_i Q_i}{W} = a_i \left(\frac{L^W}{S_L} \right)$$

$$(20) \qquad K_i^W = \frac{P_i Q_i}{R_i} = a_i \left(\frac{K^W}{S_K} \right)$$

Individual Country's Consumption, Production, and Patterns of Trade

Assumptions

1. There are three countries in this world economy. They are: the U.S., East, and the rest of the world.
   i. The rest of the world is assumed to have an inferior technology in the production of the second commodity.
   ii. The U.S. is assumed to have an inferior technology in the production of the third commodity.
   iii. For all other commodities, they have the same technology (i.e., as in equation 1).
2. Trade is assumed to be balanced (i.e., the value of imports equals the value of exports.
3. There are no transportation costs.
4. All countries are assumed to have the same relative endowment. That is:

$$\frac{K^{US}}{L^{US}} = \frac{K^R}{L^R} = \frac{K^E}{L^E}$$

The only difference in endowment is in the levels (i.e., total amount of factors of production).

Implications of the Assumptions

1. Since each country has at least two traded commodities, factor prices are equalized across countries.
2. Since there is full trade, at least initially, the inferior technology will not be used. Thus, only two commodities will be produced in the U.S. and the rest of the world.

3. The assumptions of exogenous factors endowment combined with the free trade assumptions imply that world production and consumption levels as well as factor rewards are the same as in Appendix A.

Income of Individual Countries

The countries differ only by the scale of their factor endowments. Thus:

$$(21) \qquad I^{US} = S_{US} \ I^W$$

$$(22) \qquad I^E = S_E \ I^W$$

$$(23) \qquad I^R = S_R \ I^W$$

where S_i denotes the ith country share of world resources.

Individual Country's Consumption of the Different Commodities

$$(24) \qquad C_i^1 = S_1 \ Q_1 = S_1 a_i \left(\frac{K^W}{S_K} \right)^{b_i} \left(\frac{L^W}{S_L} \right)^{b_i(S_L - S_K)}$$

where index 1 denotes the country and i the commodity.

The U.S. and the Rest of the World's Sectoral Employment

The economy's factor employment equation can be expressed as:

$$\frac{K^1}{L^1} = \frac{L_1^1}{L^1} \left(\frac{b_1 K_1}{(1-b_1)L_1} \right) + \left(1 - \frac{L_1^1}{L} \right) \left(\frac{b_i K_i}{(1-b_i) \ L_i} \right)$$

Substituting equations 3 and 4 into

$$\frac{b_i K_i}{(1-b_i) \ L_i}$$

and noting that

$$\frac{K^W}{L^W} = \frac{K^1}{L^1}$$

yields an expression for the sectoral demand for effective units of labor.

The Rest of the World

Sectoral Employment of Labor Services

(25) $\quad L_1^R = L^R \left(\dfrac{S_K - b_i}{S_L(b_1 - b_3)} \right)$

(26) $\quad L_3^R = L^R \left(\dfrac{(1 - b_3)(b_1 - S_K)}{S_L(b_1 - b_3)} \right)$

Sectoral Employment of Capital Services

(27) $\quad K_1^R = \left[\dfrac{S_K - b_3}{S_K(b_1 - b_3)} \right] \left(\dfrac{K^W}{L^W} \right) L^R$

(28) $\quad K_3^R = \left[\dfrac{b_1 - S_K}{S_K(b_1 - b_3)} \right] \left(\dfrac{K^W}{L^W} \right) L^R$

Sectoral Output

Substituting the sectoral employment into equation 1 yields the sectoral output.

(29) $\quad Q_1^R = L^R \left(\dfrac{S_K - b_3}{b_1 - b_3} \right) \left(\dfrac{K^W}{L^W} \dfrac{b_1}{S_K} \right)^{b_1} \left(\dfrac{1 - b_1}{S_2} \right)^{1 - b_1}$

(30) $\quad Q_3^R = L^R \left(\dfrac{b_1 - S_K}{b_1 - b_3} \right) \left(\dfrac{K^W}{L^W} \dfrac{b_3}{S_K} \right)^{b_3} \left(\dfrac{1 - b_3}{S_L} \right)^{1 - b_3}$

Net Trade Position

(31) $\quad M_1^R = C_1^R - Q_1^R =$

$$S_R \left(\dfrac{K^W}{S_K} \right)^{b_1} \left(\dfrac{L^W}{S_L} \right)^{(1 - b_1)}$$

$$\left[a_1 \left(\dfrac{L^W}{S_L} \right)^{b2(S_L - S_K) - (1 - b_1)} - b_1^{b_1}(1 - b_1)^{1 - b_1} \left(\dfrac{S_K - b_3}{b_1 - b_3} \right) \right].$$

Notice that $S_R = \dfrac{L^R}{L^W}$.

(32) $M_2^R = C_2^R = S\, a_2 \left(\dfrac{K^W}{S_K} \right)^{b2} \left(\dfrac{L^W}{S_L} \right)^{b2(SL-SK)}$

(33) $M_3^R = C_3^R - Q_3^R =$

$$S_R \left(\dfrac{K^W}{S_K} \right)^{b3} \left(\dfrac{L^W}{S_L} \right)^{(1-b3)}$$

$$a_3 \left[\left(\dfrac{L^W}{S_L} \right)^{b3(SL-SK)-(1-b3)} - b_3^{b3}(1-b_3)^{(1-b3)} \left(\dfrac{S_K - b_1}{b_1 - b_3} \right) \right].$$

The U.S.

Sectoral Employment of Labor Services

(34) $L_1^{US} = L^{US} \left(\dfrac{S_K - b_2}{S_L(b_1 - b_2)} \right)$

(35) $L_2^{US} = L^{US} \left(\dfrac{b_1 - S_K}{S_L(b_1 - b_i)} \right)$

Sectoral Employment of Capital Services

(36) $K_1^{US} = \left(\dfrac{S_K - b_2}{S_K(b_1 - b_2)} \right) \left(\dfrac{K^W}{L^W} \right) L^{US}$

(37) $K_2^{US} = \left(\dfrac{b_1 - S_K}{S_K(b_1 - b_2)} \right) \left(\dfrac{K^W}{L^W} \right) L^{US}$

Sectoral Output

(38) $Q_1^{US} = L^{US} \left(\dfrac{S_K - b_2}{b_1 - b_2} \right) \left(\dfrac{b_1 K^W}{S_K L^W} \right)^{b1} \left(\dfrac{1 - b_1}{S_L} \right)^{(1-b1)}$

(39) $Q_2^{US} = L^{US} \left(\dfrac{b_1 - S_K}{b_1 - b_2} \right) \left(\dfrac{b_2 K^W}{S_K L^W} \right)^{b2} \left(\dfrac{1 - b_2}{S_L} \right)^{(1-b2)}$

Net Trade Position

(40) $M_1^{US} = S_{US}\left(\dfrac{K^W}{S_K}\right)^{b1}\left(\dfrac{L^W}{S_L}\right)^{(1-b1)}$

$$\left[a_1\left(\dfrac{L^W}{S_L}\right)^{b1(S_L-S_K)-(1-b1)} - b_1^{b1}(1-b_1)^{(1-b1)}\right]$$

(41) $M_2^{US} = S_{US}\left(\dfrac{K^W}{S_K}\right)^{b2}\left(\dfrac{L^W}{S_L}\right)^{(1-b2)}$

$$\left[a_2\left(\dfrac{L^W}{S_L}\right)^{b2(S_L-S_K)-(1-b2)} - b_2^{b2}(1-b_2)^{(1-b2)}\right]$$

(42) $M_3^{US} = S_{US}a_3\left(\dfrac{K^W}{S_K}\right)^{b3}\left(\dfrac{L^W}{S_L}\right)^{b3(S_L-S_K)}$

The East

Sectoral Output

(43) $Q_1^E = Q_1^W - Q_1^{US} - Q_1^R = \left(\dfrac{K^W}{S_K}\right)^{b1}\left(\dfrac{L^w}{S_L}\right)^{(1-b1)}$

$$\left[a_1 - b_1^{b1}(1-b_1)^{(1-b1)}\left(S_R\left(\dfrac{S_K-b_3}{b_1-b_3}\right) + S_{US}\left(\dfrac{S_K-b_2}{b_1-b_2}\right)\right)\right]$$

(44) $Q_2^E = Q_2^W - Q_2^{US} = \left(\dfrac{K^W}{S_K}\right)^{b2}\left(\dfrac{L^W}{S_L}\right)^{(1-b2)}$

$$\left[a_2 - b_2^{b2}(1-b_2)^{(1-b2)}S_{US}\left(\dfrac{S_K-b_2}{b_1-b_2}\right)\right]$$

(45) $Q_3^E = Q_3^W - Q_3^R = \left(\dfrac{K^W}{S_K}\right)^{b3}\left(\dfrac{L^W}{S_L}\right)^{(1-b3)}$

$$\left[a_3 - b_3^{b3}(1-b_3)^{(1-b3)}S_R\left(\dfrac{S_K-b_3}{b_1-b_3}\right)\right]$$

Net Trade Position

(46) $M_1^F = C_1^F - Q_1^F = \left(\dfrac{K^W}{S_K}\right)^{b_1}\left(\dfrac{L^W}{S_L}\right)^{(1-b_1)}$

$$\left[b_1^{b_1}(1-b_1)^{(1-b_1)}\left(S_R\left(\dfrac{S_K-b_3}{b_1-b_3}\right)+S_{US}\left(\dfrac{S_K-b_2}{b_1-b_2}\right)-(1-S_E)\,a_1\right)\right]$$

(47) $M_2^F = \left(\dfrac{K^W}{S_K}\right)^{b_2}\left(\dfrac{L^W}{S_L}\right)^{(1-b_2)}$

$$\left[b_2^{b_2}(1-b_2)^{(1-b_2)}S_{US}\left(\dfrac{S_K-b_2}{b_1-b_2}\right)-(1-S_E)\,a_2\right]$$

(48) $M_3^F = \left(\dfrac{K^W}{S_K}\right)^{b_3}\left(\dfrac{L^W}{S_L}\right)^{(1-b_3)}$

$$\left[b_3^{b_3}(1-b_3)^{(1-b_3)}S_R\left(\dfrac{S_K-b_3}{b_1-b_3}\right)-(1-S_E)\,a_3\right]$$

East's Embargo on One Commodity without the Third Country Cooperation

Assumption

The embargo is modelled as zero net trade in the embargoed commodity (say, commodity 3).
Thus:

$M_3^E = 0$

$dQ_3^E = -M_3^E$

Sectoral Employment in the East

The changes in production of the third commodity will alter the resource availability to the other sectors.

(49) $dK_3^E = -\left(\dfrac{K^W}{L^W}\dfrac{S_L}{S_K}\right)^{S_L} M_3^E$

(50) $\quad dL_3^E = -\left(\dfrac{K^W}{L^W} \dfrac{S_L}{S_K} \right) M_3^E$

From the change in employment in sector 3, one can calculate the sectoral employment of labor in the other two sectors.

$$\frac{K^E - K_3^E}{L^E - L_3^E} = \left(\frac{L_1^E}{L^E - L_3^E} \right) \left(\frac{b_1 K_1}{(1-b_1)L_1} \right) + \left(1 - \frac{L_1^E}{L^E - L_3^E} \right) \left(\frac{b_2 K_2}{(1-b_2)L_2} \right)$$

which yields

(51) $\quad dL_1^E = \left(\dfrac{b_3 - b_2}{b_1 - b_2} \right) \left(\dfrac{K^W S_L}{L^W S_K} \right)^{-SK} M_3^E$

(52) $\quad dL_2^E = -(dL_3^E + dL_1^E) = \left(\dfrac{b_1 - b_3}{b_1 - b_2} \right) \left(\dfrac{K^W S_L}{L^W S_K} \right) (M_3^E)$

From equations 3 and 4, we know that

$dK_i^E = (dL_i^E)$

Change in East's Sectoral Output

$dQ_i^E = b_i \left(\dfrac{Q_i}{K_i} \right) dK_i^E + (1-b_i) \left(\dfrac{Q_i}{L_i} \right) dL_i^E$

(53) $\quad dQ_1^E = \left[b_1 \left(\dfrac{K^W S_L}{L^W S_K} \right)^{SL-SK} + (1-b_1) \right] \left(\dfrac{b_3 - b_2}{b_1 - b_2} \right) M_3^E$

(54) $\quad dQ_3^E = \left[b_2 \left(\dfrac{K^W S_L}{L^W S_K} \right)^{SL-SK} + (1-b_2) \right] \left(\dfrac{b_1 - b_3}{b_1 - b_2} \right) M_3^E$

The Rest of the World

Since East no longer trades commodity 3, the rest of the world will increase its production by the amount of East's reduction. Thus:

(55) $\quad dQ_3^R = M_3^E$

(56) $\quad dK_3^R = -dK_3^E$

(57) $\quad dK_3^R = dL_3^E$

However, since the rest of the world only produces two commodities:

(58) $\quad dL_1^R = -dL_3^R = dL_3^E$

(59) $\quad dK_3^R = -dK_3^R = dK_3^E$

the rest of the world's production of 1 will decline by:

(60) $\quad dQ_1^R = -M_3^E$

The U.S.

In the U.S., production will change to leave the level of world production unchanged.

(61) $\quad dQ_1^{US} = -(dQ_1^E + dQ_1^R)$

(62) $\quad dQ_2^{US} = -dQ_2^E.$

Thus, world production, consumption product and factor prices will remain unchanged and only the pattern of trade will change.

East's Embargo with Cooperation by the Rest of the World

The Choice of Commodity to be Embargoed

The only way the embargo may be effective is if there is cooperation from the rest of the world. In this case, both East and the rest of the world will embargo the U.S. Even in this case, the embargo is not automatically guranteed; it depends on which commodity is embargoed. To illustrate this, one only needs to consider an embargo in one of the commodities for which the U.S. has the same technology as the rest of the world (say, commodity 2).

In this case, the U.S. will increase the domestic production of the embargoed commodity and reduce production of the nonembargoed commodity (commodity 1). This will only result in a reduction in imports of the embargoed commodity and the export of the nonembargoed commodity. The opposite will result in the rest of the world. Again, as before, world price, production and consumption will not change, only the pattern of trade will. The analysis is somewhat different if East and the rest of the world embargo the commodity for which the U.S. has an inefficient technology.

Assumption

The following "inferior" U.S. technology is assumed.

(63) $Q_3^{US} = e(b_3 K_3^{US})^{bc} [(1-b_3) L_3^{US}]^{(1-b_3)}$

where e is an efficiency factor and is assumed to be between zero and unity.

Implications of the Previous Assumption

Since the U.S. is engaged in free trade in the other two commodities, factor prices will be equalized. Thus, based on the above production function, the U.S. price of the embargoed commodity will be:

(64) $P_3^{US} = \dfrac{P_3}{e}$

and the change in price faced by the U.S. economy:

(65) $dP_3^{US} \left(\dfrac{1-e}{e} \right) P_3$

From the demand equation

$$C_3^{US} = a_3 \left(\dfrac{I^{US}}{P_3^{US}} \right) = \left(\dfrac{a_3 S_{US}}{P_3^{US}} \right) I^W$$

(66) $dC_3^{US} = -a_3 S_{US} \left(\dfrac{K^W}{S_K} \right)^{SK} \left(\dfrac{L^W}{S_L} \right)^{1-SK} (1-e)$

The new U.S. consumption level is:

(67) $C_3^{US} = e\, a_3\, S_{US} \left(\dfrac{K^W}{S_K} \right)^{SK} \left(\dfrac{L^W}{S_L} \right)^{1-SK}$

The level of employment in industry 3 will be:

(68) $K_3^{US} = a_3 \, S_{US} \left(\dfrac{K^W}{S_K} \right)$

(69) $L_3^{US} = a_3 \, S_{US} \left(\dfrac{L^W}{S_K} \right)$

The change in sectoral employment in industries 1 and 2

(70) $dL_1^{US} = - \left(\dfrac{a_3 S_{US} \, (1 - b_1)}{(b_1 - b_2)} \right) \left(\dfrac{L^W}{S_L} \right)$

(71) $dL_2^{US} = - (L_3^{US} + dL_1^{US}) = a_3 S_{US} \left(\dfrac{L^W}{S_L} \right) \left(\dfrac{1 - b_2}{b_1 - b_2} \right)$

(72) $dK_1^{US} = dL_1^{US}$

(73) $dK_2^{US} = dL_2^{US}$

The changes in the U.S. sectoral output are:

$$dQ_i^{US} = - b_i \left(\dfrac{K^W}{L^W} \dfrac{S_L}{S_K} \right)^{S_L} + \left(\dfrac{K^W}{L^W} \dfrac{S_L}{S_K} \right)^{S_K} (1 - b_i) \, dL_i^{US}$$

(74) $dQ_1^{US} = - \left[b_1 \left(\dfrac{K^W}{L^W} \dfrac{S_L}{S_K} \right)^{S_L} + (1 - b_1) \left(\dfrac{K^W}{L^W} \dfrac{S_L}{S_K} \right) \right]$

$$\left(\dfrac{a_3 S_{US}(1 - b_1)}{(b_1 - b_2)} \right) \left(\dfrac{L^W}{S_L} \right)$$

(75) $dQ_2^{US} = a_3 S_{US} \left(\dfrac{1 - b_2}{b_1 - b_2} \right) \left(\dfrac{L^W}{S_L} \right) \left[b_2 \left(\dfrac{K^W}{L^W} \dfrac{S_L}{S_K} \right)^{S_L} + \right.$

$$\left. (1 - b_2) \left(\dfrac{K^W}{L^W} \dfrac{S_L}{S_K} \right) \right]$$

East's consumption and prices remain unchanged. East's change in production will be $-dQ_i^{US}$. The cost of the embargo to the U.S. is:

(76) $E = (1 - e) \, a_3 \, S_{US} \, I^W$

$$=(1-e) \; a_3 \; S_{US}\left(\frac{K^W}{S_K}\right)^{S_K}\left(\frac{L^W}{S_L}\right)^{S_L}$$

APPENDIX C: SOLUTION TO THE EFFECTS OF AN EMBARGO ON THE WORLDWIDE EQUILIBRIUM PRICES, OUTPUT, AND PATTERNS OF TRADE—WHEN THE INDUSTRY'S CAPITAL IS IN PLACE

Worldwide Equilibrium

Assumption

Labor is assumed to be freely mobile while the amount of capital that each sector uses is assumed to be fixed.

Implications of the Previous Assumption

Since labor is freely mobile, there will be a unique wage rate. On the other hand, since capital is fixed across industries, the return to capital will differ across sectors.

Analytically, the mobility of capital assumption is equivalent to assuming three types of capitals. Thus, the factors employment condition can be expressed as:

(1) $L^W = L_1^W + L_2^W + L_3^W$

(2) $\bar{K}_1^W = K_1^W$

(3) $\bar{K}_2^W = K_2^W$

(4) $\bar{K}_3^W = K_3^W$

Factor Rewards

From the numeraire equation, one can define the average payment to capital services.

(5) $1 = W^{S_L} \; R_1^{a_1 b_1} \; R_2^{a_2 b_2} \; R_3^{a_3 b_3}$

Thus:

(6) $R = R_1^{d_1} R_2^{d_2} R_3^{d_3}$

where $d_i = (a_i b_i)/S_K$ and $d_1 + d_2 + d_3 = 1$.

World Income

As before, one can express labor and capital share of world income as:

$$L^W = S_L \frac{I^W}{W}$$

$$K^W = S_K \frac{I^W}{W}$$

Thus:

$$\frac{W}{R} = \left(\frac{K^W}{L^W} \frac{S_L}{S_{US}} \right)$$

and

$$I^W = \left(\frac{K^W}{S_K} \right)^{S_K} \left(\frac{L^W}{S_L} \right)^{S_L}$$

$$a_i = \frac{P_i C_i^W}{I^W}$$

$$b_i = \frac{R_i (b_i K_i)}{P_i Q_i}$$

Combining the previous two equations yields:

(7) $R_i = \dfrac{P_i Q_i}{K_i^W} = \dfrac{a_i I^W}{K_i^W} = \left(\dfrac{K^W}{S_K} \right)^{S_K} \left(\dfrac{L^W}{S_L} \right)^{S_L} \left(\dfrac{K_i^W}{a_i} \right)^{-1}$

From the numeraire equation:

$$W = R_1^{\frac{-a_1b_1}{S_L}} \; R_2^{\frac{-a_2b_2}{S_L}} \; R_3^{\frac{-a_3b_3}{S_L}}$$

$$(8) \quad W = \left[\left(\frac{K_1^W}{a_1} \right)^{\frac{a_1b_1}{S_2}} \left(\frac{K_2^W}{a_2} \right)^{\frac{a_2b_2}{S_2}} \left(\frac{K_3^W}{a_3} \right)^{\frac{a_3b_3}{S_2}} \right.$$

$$\left. \left(\frac{K^W}{S_K} \right)^{S_K} \left(\frac{L^W}{S_L} \right)^{S_L} \right]^{-\frac{S_K}{S_L}}$$

Product Prices

Substituting equations 7 and 8 with the cost function yields:

$$(9) \quad P_1 = \left(\frac{K_1^W}{a_1} \right)^{\frac{-b_1}{S_L}(S_L - a_1(1-b_1))} \left(\frac{K_2^W}{a_2} \right)^{\frac{a_2b_2(1-b_1)}{S_L}}$$

$$\left(\frac{K_3^W}{a_3} \right)^{\frac{a_3b_3(1-b_1)}{S_L}} \left[\left(\frac{K^W}{S_K} \right)^{S_K} \left(\frac{L^W}{S_L} \right)^{S_L} \right]^{\frac{b_1 - S_K}{S_L}}$$

$$(10) \quad P_2 = \left(\frac{K_1^W}{a_1} \right)^{\frac{a_1b_1(1-b_2)}{S_L}} \left(\frac{K_2^W}{a_2} \right)^{\frac{-b_2}{S_L}(S_L - a_2(1-b_2))}$$

$$\left(\frac{K_3^W}{a_3} \right)^{a_3b_3(1-b_2)} \left[\left(\frac{K^W}{S_K} \right)^{S_K} \left(\frac{L^W}{S_L} \right)^{S_L} \right]^{\frac{b_2 - S_K}{S_L}}$$

$$(11) \quad P_3 = \left(\frac{K_1^W}{a_1} \right)^{\frac{a_1b_1(1-b_3)}{S_L}} \left(\frac{K_2^W}{a_2} \right)^{\frac{a_2b_2(1-b_3)}{S_L}}$$

$$\left(\frac{K_3^W}{a_3} \right)^{\frac{-b_3}{S_L}(S_L - a_3(1-b_3))} \left[\left(\frac{K^W}{S_K} \right)^{S_K} \left(\frac{L^W}{S_L} \right)^{S_L} \right]^{\frac{b_3 - S_K}{S_L}}$$

Embargo with Cooperation

Assumption

Since the third country cooperates, the solution will be analytically the same as that of a two-country world.

Factor Rewards

Since labor is free to move, there will be a single world wage rate. This and the numeraire equation imply that the average return to capital will be the same in both countries, that is:

$$(12) \qquad R^{US} = R^E$$

Thus, the absolute level of worldwide production, consumption and average return to capital are the same as those determined in the previous section.

As before, the embargo is modelled as zero trade in commodity 3. Thus, in each country the domestic production of the embargoed commodity will equal the domestic consumption and, as a result, one can solve for the return to capital employed in that sector.

$$(13) \qquad R_3^{US} = \frac{P_3^{US} Q_3^{US}}{K_3^{US}} = \frac{a_3 S_{US} I^W}{K_3^{US}}$$

$$= S_{US} \left(\frac{K^W}{S_K} \right)^{S_K} \left(\frac{L^W}{S_L} \right)^{S_L} \left(\frac{K_3^{US}}{a_3} \right)^{-1}$$

Similarly for East:

$$(14) \qquad R_3^E = S_E \left(\frac{K^W}{S_K} \right)^{S_K} \left(\frac{L^W}{S_L} \right)^{S_L} \left(\frac{K_3^E}{a_3} \right)^{-1}$$

It is interesting to point out that the world average return to R_3^W remains unchanged. That is:

$$(15) \qquad R_3^W = \left(\frac{K^W}{S_K} \right)^{S_K} \left(\frac{L^W}{S_L} \right)^{S_L} \left(\frac{K_3^W}{a^3} \right)^{-1}$$

Thus, the return to capital employed in sector 3 depends on the following conditions:

$$(16) \qquad \frac{R_3^1}{R_3^W} = S_i\left(\frac{K_3^W}{K_3^1}\right)$$

Whether the return increases, depends on whether the country's share of world income is larger than the country's share of world capital employed in that sector. Alternatively stated, if the country is a net importer, the return will increase.

Notice also that since the average return to capital, R, remains unchanged in every country, the return to other forms of capital will, on average, change to offset the change in R_3^1. Substituting for R_3^1 in R yields:

$$R_1^{(1-d3)}\left(\frac{R_2}{R_1}\right)^{d2} = \left(\frac{K^W}{S_K}\right)^{-(SL+d3SK)}\left(\frac{L^W}{S_L}\right)^{(1-d3)SL}\left(\frac{K_3^1}{a_3}\right)^{d3}\left(\frac{1}{S_1}\right)^{d3}$$

If the relative prices of the two traded commodities are the same, then:

$$\frac{R_2^1}{R_1^1} = \frac{R_1^W}{R_2^W}$$

Thus

$$\frac{R_2^1}{R_1^1} = \frac{K_1^W}{a_1}\frac{a_2}{K_2^W}$$

Substituting into the previous equation, one can then solve for R_1^1

$$(17) \qquad R_1^E = \left(\frac{K^W}{S_K}\right)^{\frac{SL-d3}{1-d3}}\left(\frac{L^W}{S_L}\right)^{SL}\left(\frac{K_3^E}{a_3}\frac{1}{S_{US}}\right)^{\frac{d3}{1-d3}}$$

$$\left(\frac{K_2^W}{K_1^W}\frac{a_1}{a_2}\right)^{\frac{d2}{1-d3}}$$

$$(18) \quad R_2^E = \left(\frac{K^W}{S_K}\right)^{\frac{S_L - d_3}{1 - d_3}} \left(\frac{L^W}{S_L}\right)^{S_L} \left(\frac{K_3^{US}}{a_3}\frac{1}{S_{US}}\right)^{\frac{d_3}{1 - d_3}}$$

$$\left(\frac{K_2^W}{K_1^W}\frac{a_1}{a_2}\right)^{-\left(\frac{1 - d_1}{1 - d_3}\right)}$$

$$(19) \quad R_1^{US} = \left(\frac{K^W}{S_K}\right)^{\frac{S_L - d_3}{1 - d_3}} \left(\frac{L^W}{S_L}\right)^{S_L} \left(\frac{K_3^R}{a_3}\frac{1}{S_{US}}\right)^{\frac{d_3}{1 - d_3}}$$

$$\left(\frac{K_2^W}{K_1^W}\frac{a_1}{a_2}\right)^{\frac{d_2}{1 - d_3}}$$

$$(20) \quad R_2^{US} = \left(\frac{K^W}{S_K}\right)^{\frac{S_L - d_3}{1 - d_3}} \left(\frac{L^W}{S_L}\right)^{S_L} \left(\frac{K_3^R}{a_3}\frac{1}{S_{US}}\right)^{\frac{d_3}{1 - d_3}}$$

$$\left(\frac{K_2^W}{K_1^W}\frac{a_1}{a_2}\right)^{\left(-\frac{1 - d_1}{1 - d_3}\right)}$$

World Sectoral Production

$$Q_i^W = C_i = a_i \frac{I^W}{P_i}$$

$$(21) \quad Q_1^W = \left(a_1\frac{K_1^W}{a_1}\right)^{\frac{-b_1\ (S_L - a_1(1 - b_1))}{S_L}} \left(\frac{K_2^W}{a_2}\right)^{a_2 b_2(1 - b_1)}$$

$$\left(\frac{K_3^W}{a_3}\right)^{a_3b_3(1-b_3)} \left[\left(\frac{K^W}{S_K}\right)^{S_K}\left(\frac{L^W}{S_L}\right)^{S_L}\right]^{\frac{1-b_2}{S_L}}$$

(22) $\quad Q_2^W = a_2\left(\frac{K_1^W}{a_1}\right)^{\frac{a_1b_1(1-b_2)}{S_L}} \left(\frac{K_2^W}{a_2}\right)^{\frac{-b_2(S_L-a_2(1-b_2))}{S_L}}$

$$\left(\frac{K_3^W}{a_3}\right)^{a_3b_3(1-b_2)} \left[\left(\frac{K^W}{S_K}\right)^{S_K}\left(\frac{L^W}{S_L}\right)^{S_L}\right]^{\frac{1-b_2}{S_L}}$$

(23) $\quad Q_3^W = a_3\left(\frac{K_1^W}{a_1}\right)^{\frac{a_1b_1(1-b_3)}{S_L}} \left(\frac{K_2^W}{a_2}\right)^{\frac{a_2b_2(1-b_3)}{S_L}}$

$$\left(\frac{K_3^W}{a_3}\right)^{\frac{-b_3\ (S_L-a_3(1-b_3))}{S_L}} \left[\left(\frac{K^W}{S_K}\right)^{S_K}\left(\frac{L^W}{S_L}\right)\right]^{\frac{1-b_3}{S_L}}$$

Price

(24) $\quad P_3^E = \left(\frac{K^W}{S_K}\right)^{S_K}\left(\frac{L^W}{S_L}\right)^{[(1-b_3)S_K+b_3S_L]} \qquad \left(\frac{K_3^E}{a_3}\right)^{-b_3}\left(S_E\right)^{b_3}$

(25) $\quad P_3^{US} = \left(\frac{K^W}{S_K}\right)\ \left(\frac{L^W}{S_L}\right)^{[(1-b_3)S_K+b_3S_L]} \qquad \left(\frac{K_3^E}{a_3}\right)^{-b_3}\left(S_{US}\right)^{b_3}$

$$(26) \quad P_2^E = \left(\frac{K^W}{S_K}\right)^{\frac{1-d_3-b_1}{1-d_3}} \left(\frac{L^W}{S_L}\right)^{[S_L b_1 + S_K(1-b_1)]}$$

$$\left(\frac{K_3^E}{a_3 S_{US}}\right)^{\frac{-d_3 b_1}{1-d_3}} \left(\frac{K_2^W}{K_1^W}\frac{a_1}{a_2}\right)^{\frac{-d_2 b_1}{1-d_3}}$$

$$(27) \quad P_2^{US} = \left(\frac{K^W}{S_K}\right)^{\frac{1-d_3-b_1}{1-d_3}} \left(\frac{L^W}{S_L}\right)^{-[S_L b_1 + S_K(1-b_1)]}$$

$$\left(\frac{K_3^{US}}{a_3 S_{US}}\right)^{\frac{-d_3 b_1}{1-d_3}} \left(\frac{K_2^W}{K_1^W}\frac{a_1}{a_2}\right)^{\frac{-d_2 b_1}{1-d_3}}$$

$$(28) \quad P_1^E = \left(\frac{K^W}{S_K}\right)^{\frac{1-d_3-b_2}{1-d_3}} \left(\frac{L^W}{S_L}\right)^{S_L b_2 + S_K(1-b_2)}$$

$$\left(\frac{K_3^E}{a_3 S_R}\right)^{\frac{-d_3 b_2}{1-d_3}} \left(\frac{K_2^W}{K_1^W}\frac{a_1}{a_2}\right)^{\frac{-d_2 b_2}{1-d_3}}$$

$$(29) \quad P_1^{US} = \left(\frac{K^W}{S_K}\right)^{\frac{1-d_3-b_2}{1-d_3}} \left(\frac{L^W}{S_L}\right)^{-S_L b_2 + S_K(1-b_2)}$$

$$\left(\frac{K_3^{US}}{a_3 S_{US}}\right)^{\frac{-d_3 b_2}{1-d_3}} \left(\frac{K_2^W}{K_1^W}\frac{a_1}{a_2}\right)^{\frac{-d_2 b_2}{1-d_3}}$$

From this, one can now calculate the consumption level of each country and compare it to the free trade solution. Given the changes in consumption, one can then calculate the change in well-being due to the embargo. Notice that even though the countries, measured income does not change, well-being will.

$$C_i = a_i \frac{I^w}{P_i}$$

4

The Sectoral Impact of Trade Policies: The Net Benefits and Costs to the Various Sectors of the U.S. Economy*

Trade policy in the United States is, with ever greater frequency, being used to aid domestic industries. Often it is argued that the costs of trade restraints to the overall economy are small relative to the benefits to be derived from protecting given industry. The economic (and political) cost of layoffs centered in a particular industry and region, for example, are portrayed as being greater than the less easily identified "theoretical" costs imposed on the rest of the economy by trade restrictions. But, trade restrictions improperly applied may hurt, rather than help a domestic industry. Moreover, unless the restrictions are permanent, and thereby capable of altering the competitiveness of an industry over the entire horizon of its investments, they can be expected to have no permanent effect on an industry. A temporary restriction may provide temporary relief from competition. But, in the absence of other fundamental changes, once that protection is lifted, the industry's health most likely will revert to where it was before restraints were imposed.

This chapter presents four case studies analyzing the effectiveness of trade policies used to aid a domestic industry. First, the apparently successful case of temporary import restraints on color televisions is explored.

*Portions of Chapter 4 are based on Victor A. Canto and Arthur B. Laffer, "The Incidence of Trade Restriction," *Columbia Journal of World Business,* 17, no. 1 (Spring 1982): 60–66. Victor A. Canto, Richard V. Eastin, and Arthur B. Laffer, "Failure of Protectionism: A Study of the Steel Industry," *Columbia Journal of World Business* 17, no. 4 (Winter 1982): 43–57. Reprinted with permission. Victor A. Canto and Arthur B. Laffer, "The Effectiveness of Orderly Marketing Agreements: The Color TV Case," *Business Economics* 18, no. 1 (January 1983): 38–45. Reprinted with permission of the National Association of Business Economists.

Second, the more complex, and apparently unsuccessful, attempt to assist the domestic steel industry adjust to foreign competition is presented. Third, the factors contributing to the current increase in the market share of foreign automobiles in the U.S. market are analyzed. The likely impact of the restraints on the imports of Japanese autos is then presented. Fourth and finally, the politically motivated, and apparently unsuccessful, U.S. export embargo on shipments of superphosphoric acid to the Soviet Union is analyzed.

CASE I: TEMPORARY IMPORT RESTRAINTS ON COLOR TELEVISIONS

In the spring of 1977, an Orderly Marketing Agreement (OMA) on color televisions was negotiated between the governments of the United States and Japan. The agreement was partially in response to a petition filed with the International Trade Commission by a group of labor unions and some smaller firms in the electronics industry in response to a rapid increase in the Japanese penetration of the lucrative color TV market.

The success of the Japanese in the color TV market was viewed as a threat to one of the last areas where domestic manufacturers were able to compete in the consumer electronic market. By 1978, 100 percent of household radios, 90 percent of CB radios, and 85 percent of black and white TVs were imported (Table 4.1). By contrast, only 18 percent of the domestic color TV market was supplied by imports.

Japanese color TV exports to the United States had increased to 2.5 million units in 1976 from just 1.2 million units in 1971. The agreement, which became effective in mid-1977, lasted three years and called for the government of Japan to restrain exports of complete color televisions into the United States to 1.56 million units per year, and of "incomplete" sets to 190,000 per year. Thus, the Orderly Marketing Agreement was, in essence, an import quota. The situation created by the Orderly Marketing Agreement with the Japanese regarding color TVs can be analyzed within a three-country, international trade framework.[1] In this particular case, capital and labor are free to move within a country, but cannot move across national boundaries, and there are at least two countries capable of producing the product being analyzed. Under these conditions, when the imports of a commodity or product from one country are restricted, imports from the country decline—but resources shift in the rest of the world to produce the restricted product in order to meet the demand in

TABLE 4.1. Import Penetration in Consumer Electronics, 1978*

Product	Imports as Percent of U.S. Consumption
Video players/records	100%
Household radios	100
CB radios	90
Black and white TVs	85
Electronic watches	68
High fidelity and stereo components	64
Phonographs and compact stereo systems	43
Audio tape recorders	35
Microwave ovens	25
Color TVs	18

*The table understates the significance of imports because many products assembled in the United States are counted as domestic production and include substantial foreign value added. This does not only include components and subassemblies such as circuit boards, but complete chassis are often imported.

Source: "The U.S. Consumer Electronics Industry and Foreign Competition, Executive Summary," final report under EDA grant No. 06–07002–10. Department of Commerce. Economic Development Administration, May 1980, p. 2.

the newly opened market. The net result is a shift in trade patterns, with no impact on total output or employment in any of the three countries involved.

The initial response of producers inside and outside the U.S. after the imposition of the Orderly Marketing Agreement for Japanese-produced color TVs is consistent with this description. Imports of color TVs from Japan fell sharply—declining from a peak of 2.5 million units in 1976, the last complete year before imposition of the trade restrictions, to 1.4 million units in 1978. But color TV imports from the rest of the world, particularly Taiwan and Korea, rose sharply. Table 4.2 shows that the net result was that nearly the same number of color TVs were imported in 1978 as in 1976 (Fig. 4.1).

Pressures were now created for new orderly marketing agreements to be negotiated with Taiwan and Korea. In 1980, imports from these two countries were limited to 526,000 units for the year ending June 30, 1980. For the following year, exports from each of these two countries were permitted to rise to one million units.

The restrictions on color TV imports appear to have worked. Total

TABLE 4.2. Color TVs—U.S. Imports by Quantity Totals and by Country of Origin, 1971–80 (In Thousands of Units)

Period	Total	Japan	Taiwan	Korea	Singapore	Canada	Other
1971	1,281	1,191	85	—	—	4	1
1972	1,318	1,094	213	10	—	—	1
1973	1,399	1,059	325	2	—	1	12
1974	1,282	916	337	2	—	1	6
1975	1,215	1,044	143	22	—	2	4
1976	2,834	2,530	235	48	4	15	2
1977	2,539	2,029	322	97	15	74	2
1978	2,775	1,424a	624	437	61	212	7
1979	1,369	513	367	314	73	91	2
1980	1,275	424	303	292	85	124	2

aImports from Japan during the first OMA restraint year (the last two quarters of 1977 and the first two quarters of 1978) were 1.63 million complete units.

Source: U.S. Bureau of the Census, Table 1 TSUSA Commodity by Country of Origin.

FIGURE 4.1. Color Television Imports By Country of Origin, 1971–80

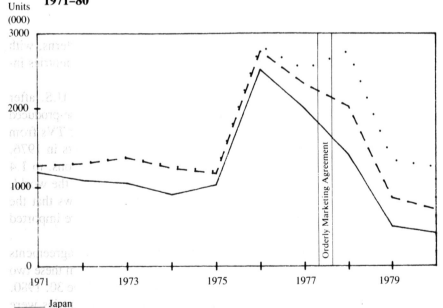

——— Japan
– – – Japan and Korea
. . . . . Total color television imports (Japan, Korea, Taiwan, Singapore, Canada, Other)

Source: Effects of Restrictions on United States Imports.

imports fell, and at the same time (1977–80), production of color TVs in the U.S. jumped 3 million units to 10 million sets (Table 4.3).

However, appearances are deceiving. Behind the overall numbers is the virtually complete circumvention of the trade restrictions. Instead of importing complete TVs, both U.S. and foreign-owned domestic producers

TABLE 4.3. U.S. Production of Complete Color Television Receivers

	Period	Thousands of Units
1977	1st Quarter	1,608
	2nd Quarter	1,824
	3rd Quarter	1,697
	4th Quarter	1,875
	Total	7,004
1978	1st Quarter	1,905
	2nd Quarter	2,126
	3rd Quarter	2,069
	4th Quarter	2,182
	Total	8,282
1979	1st Quarter	2,147
	2nd Quarter	2,208
	3rd Quarter	2,106
	4th Quarter	2,551
	Total	9,012
1980	1st Quarter	2,661
	2nd Quarter	2,724
	3rd Quarter	2,486
	4th Quarter	2,789
	Total	10,660
1981	1st Quarter	2,835
	2nd Quarter	2,770
	3rd Quarter	2,523
	4th Quarter	2,386
	Total	10,514

Source: "Color Television Receivers: U.S. Production, Shipments, Inventories, Exports, Employment, Man-Hours, and Prices," 1978–81, United States International Trade Commission, Washington, D.C.

began production of the TVs in the U.S., then exported the incomplete set for additional assembly including the use of foreign-manufactured components, then "reimported" the TVs for final assembly. Reimported TVs are not covered by the trade restricitons. This route around the trade restrictions was facilitated both by special tax provisions provided by foreign countries, and a special provision in U.S. tariff codes.[2] Taiwan, Korea and Mexico in particular provide special tax advantages for the manufacture of consumer electronic products, including TVs, that, along with competitive labor rates, attract the subproduction of color TVs for the U.S. parts market. Under the tariff codes, if a U.S. firm ships color television parts abroad for assembly, then reimports the still-incomplete TVs, only the value added is subject to a 5 percent tariff. Foreign companies that avoid the Orderly Marketing Agreement restrictions by selling parts and performing subassembly operations for foreign companies may also own the American company for whom they are doing the work. Symmetrically, domestic companies may locate facilities outside the U.S. where parts are manufactured and combined into subassemblies. Given the cost and tax advantages of locating production facilities outside the U.S., the 5 percent tariff is not high enough to prevent this adjustment to trade patterns. If everything else is the same, this route around the Orderly Marketing Agreement would be expected to add a maximum of 5 percent to the original cost of the television.

During the 1977-80 period, incomplete color TV imports rose to nearly 3 million units from virtually zero in 1976, the year before imports were restricted (Table 4.4). Subtracting these units from total "U.S.-produced" TVs indicates that the domestic production of color TVs has increased only slightly since the imposition of the Orderly Marketing Agreement. Moreover, since 1977, the number of persons employed and the average number of man-hours worked in the domestic industry have declined (Table 4.5).

The analysis suggests that, at best, the Orderly Marketing Agreement has created employment only for those people assembling the television sets in the U.S., which is only a fraction of the labor force employed in the production of color televisions. The Orderly Marketing Agreement amounted, first, to an import quota exclusively on Japan, then on Korea and Taiwan as well. To the extent these quotas were circumvented, the outlook for the profitability of U.S. producers of color TVs would be expected to remain relatively unchanged. Indeed, a comparison of the stock price movements of Japanese and U.S. companies intensive in the production of color TVs (including Zenith, RCA and Motorola domestically, and

TABLE 4.4.   Imports of Incomplete Color Television Receivers, Quarterly in Units

Period		Total for the World	Japan	Taiwan	Mexico
1977*	3rd Quarter	236,793	61,082	34,481	136,249
	4th Quarter	309,419	47,217	102,137	157,342
	Total	546,212	108,299	136,618	293,591
1978	1st Quarter	389,046	43,131	128,916	214,898
	2nd Quarter	620,335	47,999	215,410	347,699
	3rd Quarter	561,877	54,850	297,638	206,039
	4th Quarter	572,036	75,016	214,122	276,831
	Total	2,143,294	220,996	856,086	1,045,467
1979		Not available			
1980**	Total	2,734,743	81,548	335,380	1,597,231

 * 3rd and 4th quarter data only
 ** Quarterly data not available
 Source: U.S. Bureau of the Census.

TABLE 4.5.   Average Number of Persons Employed and Man-Hours Worked in the Production of Color Television Receivers, Annually 1977–81

	Number Employed		Man-Hours in Thousands	
Period	All Persons	Production and Related Workers	All Persons	Production and Related Workers
1977	29,104	24,976	59,442	50,355
1978	27,593	23,855	56,987	48,292
1979	26,190	22,470	54,272	44,433
1980	24,859	21,678	51,480	44,592
1981	21,773	18,751	43,980	37,755

Source: "Color Television Receivers: U.S. Production. Shipments, Inventories, Imports, Employment. Man-Hours, and Prices," 1978–81, United States Trade Commission, Washington, D.C. Table 5.

Sony and Matsushita in Japan), indicates no systematic increase in the market value of the U.S. firms relative to their Japanese counterparts during the three months the Orderly Marketing Agreement became effective (Fig. 4.2). This result is consistent with the evidence presented in this section. That is, import quotas on color TVs have had little impact on the U.S. economy. But even after the agreement was allowed to lapse in mid-1980, there was no systematic benefit evident for U.S. companies.

To the extent the Orderly Marketing Agreement has shifted the location of production facilities around the world, however, it may have distributed profits away from Japan, then Korea and Taiwan, toward countries that are not parties to the agreements. Such countries in particular would include Mexico and Canada, which have increased significantly their production of color TVs and color TV components.

FIGURE 4.2. Monthly Stock Price Performance of Major Color TV Manufacturers, 1977–80

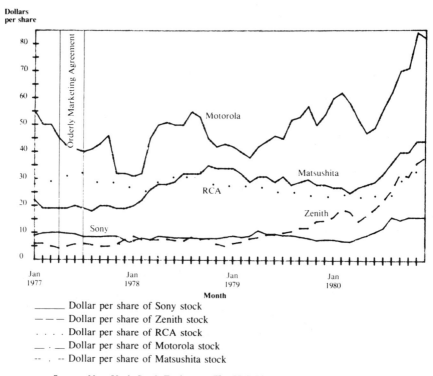

_____ Dollar per share of Sony stock
– – – Dollar per share of Zenith stock
. . . . . Dollar per share of RCA stock
__ . __ Dollar per share of Motorola stock
-- . -- Dollar per share of Matsushita stock

Source: New York Stock Exchange. _The SRC Blue Book of 3-Trend Cycli-Graphs._

Effects of the Color TV Orderly Marketing Agreement

The effects of the Orderly Marketing Agreement on production and sales of color televisions include:

Changing patterns of trade. Imports of finished color televisions shifted away from the country subject to the Orderly Marketing Agreement (Japan) to countries that were not subject to the OMA (Taiwan, Korea and Canada).

Changing the composition of imports. The OMA reduced the imports of complete color televisions. But the effect of this restriction was almost completely offset by the "reimportation" on incomplete TVs.

Leaving the price of color TVs virtually unchanged. Evidence of the ineffectiveness of these restrictions is that they have had no significant effect on the price of color televisions (Table 4.6). The color TV price index indicates a price increase of less than the 5 percent tariff levied on the value added of imported components.

Leaving total U.S. production virtually unchanged. Foreign producers have set up plants in the U.S., but the impact of these plants on overall U.S. production and employment is virtually nil. These plants assemble parts components and subassemblies, virtually all of which are imported. Assembly is but a small part of overall TV production. Still, TVs assembled in these plants are counted as "U.S.-produced." Thus, the appar-

**TABLE 4.6. Price Index for Televisions
(Color and Monochrome Combined)
from the Consumer Price Index (CPI), Monthly 1976–81 (1967 = 100)**

Month	1981	1980	1979	1978	1977	1976
Jan.	105.6	103.7	102.9	101.1	102.8	103.0
Feb.	105.7	103.7	102.9	101.0	102.4	103.1
March	105.6	104.0	103.0	101.4	102.2	103.1
April	106.0	104.0	103.0	101.5	101.9	103.1
May	105.4	104.1	102.8	101.3	101.6	103.1
June	105.3	104.2	102.7	101.2	101.4	102.8
July	105.6	104.4	102.6	101.3	101.2	102.7
Aug.	105.0	105.0	102.8	101.5	101.2	102.6
Sept.	104.6	105.0	102.9	101.9	101.4	102.9
Oct.	105.0	104.7	103.4	102.1	101.5	102.6
Nov.	104.8	105.1	103.6	102.4	101.5	103.0
Dec.	104.7	105.2	103.6	102.7	101.2	102.9
Average for year	105.3	104.4	103.0	101.6	101.7	102.9

ent increase in U.S. production of color TVs represents nothing more than the shifting of the final assembly of components to the U.S. from outside the U.S. Although American-owned firms retain the major share of the domestic color television market, much of their production also has been relocated to foreign countries. Weaker U.S. manufacturers of television and other consumer electronic goods have disappeared. Total U.S. employment in color TVs has declined.

The markets have continuously found an inexpensive way (the cost is 5 percent of the value added) to avoid the U.S. restrictions on the imports of consumer electronic products. The evidence suggests that the import restrictions imposed on color TVs have had no major effect on color television prices, employment or output in the U.S.

CASE II: VOLUNTARY RESTRAINT AGREEMENTS AND THE STEEL INDUSTRY

In 1969, the first Voluntary Restraint Agreements (VRAs) were negotiated with Japanese and European exporters in an effort to stem the steadily growing market share of Japanese steel imports. The VRAs expired in 1974. In 1978, trigger prices—a form of minimum price for imported steel based on the Japanese steel industry's production costs—were imposed. Petitions filed early in 1982 by U.S. steel companies against European and other foreign countries while the trigger-pricing mechanism was still in effect were stark testimony to the failure of protectionism to revitalize the domestic steel industry.

Prior to the 1960s, tariffs on steel products averaged just 6 to 8 percent of the value of imports. Nontariff barriers were insignificant, yet imports of steel products into the U.S. were inconsequential. During the 1950s, transportation costs acted as a barrier to Japanese imports. However, Japanese efficiency continued to improve while the comparative advantage of U.S. producers diminished.

This natural protection, which permitted price increases in excess of unit-cost increases, began to disappear in 1959, when the industry chose to endure a strike rather than pass on higher labor costs to steel consumers. It is important to note that the 1959 strike only facilitated the "sudden" penetration of Japanese steel into the U.S. market. The arrival of Japanese steel on U.S. shores was an event long in the making.[3]

By 1959, the U.S. comparative advantage in bar, structural and possibly plate steel had been eroded completely (Fig. 4.3). By 1963, the Jap-

FIGURE 4.3. Prices of Domestic and Imported Carbon Steel Products

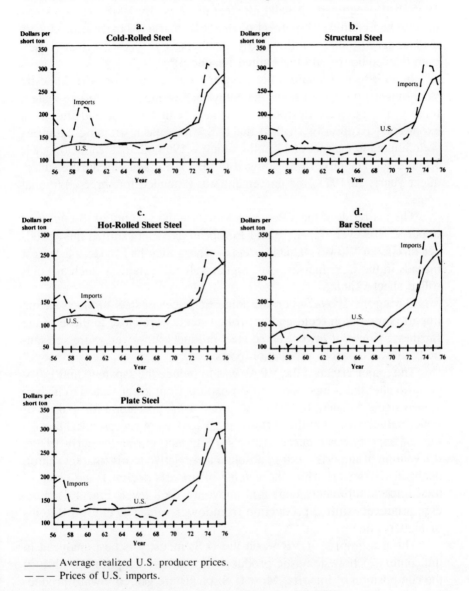

_____ Average realized U.S. producer prices.

— — — Prices of U.S. imports.

Source: The U.S. Steel Industry in Recurrent Crisis, Crandall (1981).

anese had overtaken the U.S. in almost all major steel products and, by 1965, had penetrated virtually all steel markets. By 1968, foreign steelmakers had claimed 18 percent of the U.S. market. Japanese producers had the largest share, followed by steelmakers in West Germany, Belgium/Luxembourg and the United Kingdom.[4]

In an effort to obtain relief from foreign competition, the domestic steel industry prevailed upon the Johnson Administration to negotiate a three-year Voluntary Restraint Agreement with Japanese and European exporters.[5] Exports of steel to the U.S. from the restraining countries were limited to a target of 14 million tons in 1969—22 percent below their 1968 level. The target was allowed to increase graduallly during subsequent years. In 1971, the agreement was extended for three additional years.

The net result of the VRAs was to reduce the quantity of foreign steel imports. However, Japanese and European exporters shifted their product mix from "lower-valued" steels—where they had made the largest inroads in the U.S. market—to "higher-valued" products, such as cold-rolled sheet (Table 4.7).

During the 1969–74 period, domestic prices of steel products facing import competition (cold-and hot-rolled steel) were close to those of the Japanese. Prices of lower-valued steel products, however, were substantially above Japanese production costs.

The major effect of the VRAs was to induce the Japanese and Europeans to alter the composition of their exports from lower-valued to higher-valued steel. As such, the VRAs afforded some protection for makers of lower-valued steel. On the surface, the VRAs were successful: The volume of imports was reduced (Table 4.7). In fact, during the early 1970s, the volume of imports, both in absolute and relative terms (market share), declined. However, while the *volume* of imports declined, the *value* of total imports ultimately increased above its 1968 level (Fig. 4.4). Foreign producers shifted production from lower-valued steel toward items of higher value.[6]

The true impact of VRAs on the U.S. industry is best analyzed in the context of how domestic producers are able to adapt to this shift in the composition of imports. Most U.S. plants are geared toward production of certain types of steel, making the composition of their output relatively fixed. The analysis suggests, then, that the rate of return on higher-valued steel will decline due to increased Japanese competition. Similarly, the rate of return on lower-valued steel will increase with reduced competition. The magnitude of the effect on rates of return depends on the industry's ability to alter production from high-valued to low-valued steel.

TABLE 4.7. Carbon Steel Imports, 1956–80 (Thousands of Short Tons)

Year	Bars	Cold-rolled sheet	Hot-rolled sheet	Plate	Structurals
1956	44.6	2.7	4.0	62.1	603.6
1957	23.8	1.8	0.4	29.3	428.9
1958	78.3	0.2	6.1	27.2	299.5
1959	195.5	28.8	68.4	363.0	863.3
1960	112.3	65.8	127.3	281.6	594.0
1961	103.1	5.7	10.6	68.2	551.3
1962	113.4	54.1	51.2	204.9	684.0
1963	192.4	192.4	230.0	352.1	777.6
1964	332.4	383.6	521.9	460.3	638.2
1965	497.0	1,218.4	1,797.0	771.8	928.8
1966	500.1	1,119.7	1,946.2	943.7	946.8
1967	552.7	1,369.9	2,261.4	1,012.8	1,063.4
1968	804.9	2,825.9	3,436.5	1,755.9	1,512.7
1969	685.8	1,907.5	1,930.5	1,171.1	1,434.1
1970	527.7	2,174.9	1,997.5	944.7	1,186.2
1971	798.1	3,544.3	2,659.7	1,538.7	1,572.0
1972	791.9	3,236.2	2,231.0	1,648.3	1,712.3
1973	707.6	2,704.4	1,786.5	1,319.8	1,338.1
1974	677.5	2,547.6	1,765.0	1,693.7	1,234.7
1975	418.6	2,067.1	1,509.2	1,353.0	876.3
1976	369.1	2,350.7	1,635.9	1,555.4	1,425.0
1977	693.6	3,345.1	2,675.0	2,108.3	1,817.0
1978	587.2	3,123.4	2,613.0	2,875.0	1,926.2
1979	453.2	2,322.3	2,153.4	1,774.5	1,952.9
1980	367.7	1,415.4	1,479.4	2,028.2	1,813.2
1981	418.0	1,626.0	1,628.1	2,447.7	1,976.8
1982	297.5	1,706.7	1,355.0	1,619.5	1,483.5
1983	457.1*	2,417.2	2,316.8	1,103.2	1,444.7

*Bars total now includes all grades—carbon, alloy and stainless.

Source: For data from 1956–78, see Robert W. Crandall. The U.S. Steel Industry in Recurrent Crisis. p. 166; 1979–80 data supplied by the American Iron and Steel Institute.

To the extent that these changes are costly, the rate of return on producing high-valued steel will decline and that of low-valued steel will increase. These changes in rates of return will tend to offset each other.

Effects of the VRAs on the Steel Industry

A comparison of the steel industry's rate of return with that of all U.S. manufacturing shows that the Voluntary Restraint Agreements did little to benefit the domestic steel industry. In 1969, the year the VRAs

FIGURE 4.4. **Total Value of U.S. Imports of Carbon Steel Products, 1956–76**

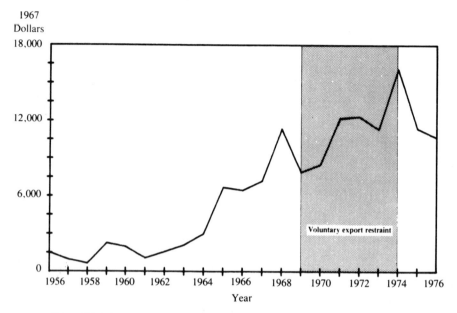

_____ Price of U.S. imported carbon steel products multiplied by thousands of short tons imported and adjusted for inflation (using CPI)

Source: The U.S. Steel Industry in Recurrent Crises, Crandall (1981).

were imposed, imports fell 22 percent. The steel industry's rate of return remained unchanged at 7.6 percent, while that for all U.S. manufacturers declined to 11.5 percent from 12.1 percent.[7] The following year, after-tax returns for the steel industry slumped to 4.3 percent (a 43 percent drop), compared with the 9.3 percent rate of return (19 percent drop) recorded by all manufacturers.[8] Beginning in 1971, the decline in the rate of return to steel manufacturing, both in absolute terms and relative to all U.S. manufacturing, reversed itself. But in 1977, the industry's rate of return declined to 3.6 percent, more than 10 percentage points below that earned by all U.S. manufacturers.

The voluntary restraint period spanned the years 1969 through 1974. The rate of return in the steel industry was lower during this period than either just before or after. Even though the rate of return on the protected, low-valued steel products did increase, the rate of return on the unprotected high-valued steel declined. Overall, the profitability of steel manufacturing declined.

Any benefit to producers of lower-valued steel came at the expense of domestic industry and American consumers who were forced to purchase the more expensive domestically produced steel. The overall effect was a deterioration in the average rate of return for the steel industry relative to all manufacturers. Thus, it is not surprising to find that, during this period, capital expenditures in constant dollars declined relative to 1967 and the years following expiration of the VRAs (Fig. 4.5).

Finally, between 1968 and 1974, employment in the steel industry fell by more than 27,000 workers (Table 4.8). The VRAs were not effective in arresting the secular decline in the industry's employment.

When the VRAs lapsed, it was evident that after six years of protection, the domestic steel industry was still at a comparative disadvantage, especially relative to Japanese steel producers. Steel imports again began to increase as a share of the U.S. market, rising to 17.8 percent in 1977. That year, the industry began asking for reinstitution of policies designed to protect it against foreign competition.

FIGURE 4.5. Capital Expenditures by U.S. Steel Industry, 1963–81

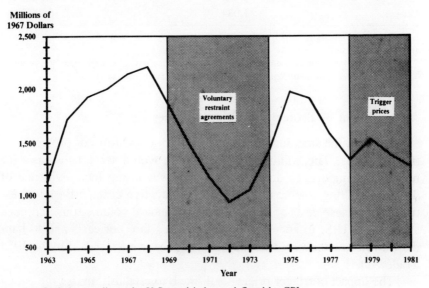

_____ Capital expenditures by U.S. steel industry deflated by CPI

Source: Annual Statistical Report, American Iron and Steel Institute.

TABLE 4.8. Employment* and Capital Expenditures in the U.S. Steel Industry, 1963–81

Year	Capital Expenditures (millions of dollars)	Average Number of Employees**
1963	$1,134	405,536
1964	1,722	434,654
1965	1,929	458,539
1966	2,008	446,712
1967	2,145	424,153
1968	2,214	420,684
1969	1,864	415,301
1970	1,493	403,115
1971	1,175	366,982
1972	937	364,074
1973	1,052	392,851
1974	1,432	393,212
1975	1,972	339,945
1976	1,908	339,021
1977	1,570	337,396
1978	1,328	339,155
1979	1,523	341,931
1980	1,373	291,483
1981	1,267	286,219
1982	1,460	198,477
1983	1,084	168,852

*Covering only those employees receiving wages engaged in the production and sale of iron and steel products.

**Average of the monthly number of employees receiving pay, after adjustment for turnover.

Source: Annual Statistical Report. American Iron and Steel Institute, 1981.

A New Form of Protection: Trigger Prices

In 1978, the steel industry was provided a new form of protection—trigger prices. This minimum price system would serve as a basis for monitoring imports to determine if there was prima facie evidence of dumping (selling steel at a price below production costs).[9] Based on estimated Japanese costs of production at a standard volume, this approach allowed the U.S. to keep European steel at "fair" prices[10] and to handle with finesse the very troubling cost-of-production standard in the 1974 Trade Act.[11]

The impact of trigger pricing is difficult to establish, in that the policy was imposed during the 1975–79 worldwide surge in steel shipments (Table 4.9). Between 1974 and 1979, there was no noticeable change in the trend for the share of world production that was exported. As a result of these changes in worldwide conditions and the recovery of the U.S. economy, both U.S. production and imports increased (Table 4.9). The rate of return for manufacturing steel also went up.

In this context, the rapid increase in imports is the result of domestic demand for steel growing more rapidly than domestic capacity to meet that demand. In an integrated world economy, it is precisely these conditions that lead to an increase in imports and a deterioration of the trade balance. Furthermore, given a fixed capital stock, one would expect a substantial increase in the rate of return for the industry.

As demand leveled out in 1980, the surge in imports subsided to a level comparable to that of the early 1970s (Table 4.9). The reduction in imports and loss of market share in 1979 cannot be attributed solely to the trigger price mechanism. With the decline in the growth in demand, rates of return would be expected to level off as well. This is precisely what happened. The increase in the rate of return implies that incentives to invest increased. The industry did respond to these incentives by increasing capital expenditures in 1979 above previous levels. As demand and rates of return subsided, capital investments declined (Fig. 4.5).

That mechanism, however, distorted trade patterns. Trigger prices, in effect, forced Japanese and European steel companies to charge a price higher than their marginal costs (profit maximizing). Between 1977 and 1980, steel prices increased by 40.5 percent while the consumer price level increased 36.1 percent. It is possible that steel prices in the U.S. may have been kept artificially high. To some extent, this helped U.S. producers. At the same time, it provided incentives to other foreign producers, such as Canada, Korea and South Africa, to enter the U.S. market (Table 4.10).

Japanese and European market share peaked at 13.5 percent in 1977. By 1980, their share had declined to 9.1 percent, but during this period, the rest-of-world share of the apparent steel supply increased from 4.3 percent to 7.2 percent. Canada's share increased approximately 50 percent to 2.5 percent of the market, while the rest-of-world share nearly doubled to 4.7 percent of the market. The net result was a meager 1.5 percent increase in the domestic industry's share of the U.S. market (Table 4.11).

Effects of the Trigger Pricing Mechanism

The results of this economic experiment can be explained by looking at the world as an integrated economy. During periods of high de-

TABLE 4.9. Steel Mill Products—U.S. Capacity, Production and Imports, and World Production and Exports, 1956–81 (Millions of Net Tons)

	United States				World		
Year	Raw Steel Capacity*	Raw Steel Production	Imports	Exports	Raw Steel Production	Exports (Raw Steel Equivalent)	Percent Exported
1956	129.9	115.2	1.3	4.2	313.4	39.5	12.6
1957	132.9	112.7	1.2	5.2	323.5	44.1	13.6
1958	136.3	85.3	1.7	2.7	302.6	41.9	13.8
1959	139.8	93.4	4.4**	1.7	337.6	46.4	13.7
1960	142.8	99.3	3.4	3.0	380.8	58.1	15.3
1961	143.6	98.0	3.2	2.0	390.5	57.7	14.3
1962	144.7	98.3	4.1**	2.0	395.4	61.7	15.5
1963	145.9	109.3	5.5	2.2	424.1	66.1	15.6
1964	147.5	127.1	6.4	3.4	478.6	76.4	16.0
1965	148.2	131.5	10.4**	2.5	503.8	86.5	17.2
1966	149.4	134.1	10.8	1.7	521.1	86.4	16.6
1967	150.6	127.2	11.5	1.7	547.8	94.4	17.2
1968	152.2	131.5	18.0**	2.2	583.9	109.1	18.7

1969	152.8	141.3	14.0	5.2	633.4	120.4	19.0
1970	153.8	131.5	13.4	7.1	656.2	129.4	19.7
VRA 1971	154.8	120.4	18.3**	2.8	642.0	138.2	21.5
period 1972	156.2	133.2	17.7	2.9	694.6	146.6	21.1
1973	156.7	150.8	15.1	4.1	769.5	161.8	21.0
1974	157.0	145.7	16.0**	5.8	781.2	187.2	24.0
1975	157.4	116.6	12.0	3.0	711.9	163.1	22.9
1976	157.7	128.0	14.3	2.7	745.0	179.7	24.1
1977	158.1	125.3	19.3**	2.0	744.5	179.7	24.1
Trigger 1978	156.0	137.0	21.1	2.4	790.6	196.3	24.8
pricing 1979	na	136.3	17.5	2.8	824.5	200.7	24.4
period 1980	na	111.8	15.5	4.1	790.4	197.1	25.0
1981	na	120.8	19.9	2.9	780.7	na	na
1982	na	74.6	16.7	1.8	711.7	na	na
1983	na	84.6	17.1	1.2	731.7	na	na

*Capacity estimates are based on peak production months according to D. F. Barnett, "The Canadian Steel Industry in a Competitive World Environment" (Ottawa: Resource Industries and Construction Branch, Industry, Trade and Commerce, 1977), vol. 2, paper 14.

**Year of expiration of labor contract.

Source: For data from 1956–79, see Robert W. Crandall, *The U.S. Steel Industry in Recurrent Crisis*, p. 24–25; 1979–83 data supplied by the American Iron and Steel Institute.

TABLE 4.10. U.S. Imports of Total Steel Mill Products By Country of Origin, 1976–83 (Thousands of Net Tons)

Country of Origin	1976	1977	1978	1979	1980	1981	1982	1983
Canada	1,303.7	1,892.0	2,363.9	2,353.9	2,369.5	2,898.8	1,844.2	2,378.6
Total Latin America	311.5	391.4	772.8	647.1	329.9	782.2	974.4	2,414.5
Total EEC	3,187.7	6,832.9	7,463.4	5,405.4	3,886.8	6,482.1	5,596.6	4,114.3
Total Europe	3,739.6	7,681.0	9,211.1	6,392.8	4,743.9	8,077.4	6,774.6	5,309.8
Japan	7,984.1	7,820.4	6,487.2	6,336.0	6,006.8	6,220.1	5,185.1	4,236.9
Korean Republic	790.5	790.0	1,052.1	985.7	1,039.9	1,218.4	1,062.1	1,727.6
Taiwan	62.5	67.2	250.4	108.5	85.9	131.2	117.6	117.2
Republic of South Africa	21.5	463.1	695.0	485.3	440.7	371.1	529.8	556.9
Australia and Oceania	49.9	105.0	180.7	159.4	131.7	128.8	130.0	206.0
Total Imports of Steel Mill Products	14,284.6	19,306.6	21,134.6	17,518.1	15,495.0	19,898.3	16,662.5	17,069.9

Source: Annual Statistical Report, American Iron and Steel Institute, 1980, Table 25, p. 49, and 1981, Table 25, p. 49.

TABLE 4.11. Steel Imports as Percent of Apparent U.S. Steel Supply,* 1971–83

Year	Total	Japan	EEC	Canada	Other
1971	17.9	6.7	7.0	1.2	3.0
1972	16.6	6.0	6.1	1.1	3.4
1973	12.4	4.6	5.3	0.9	1.6
1974	13.4	5.1	5.4	1.1	1.8
1975	13.5	6.6	4.6	1.1	1.2
1976	14.1	7.9	3.2	1.3	1.7
1977	17.8	7.2	6.3	1.7	2.6
1978	18.1	5.6	6.4	2.0	4.1
1979	15.2	5.5	4.7	2.0	3.0
1980	16.3	6.3	4.1	2.5	3.4
1981	19.1	6.0	6.2	2.8	4.1
1982	21.8	6.8	7.3	2.4	5.3
1983	20.5	5.1	4.9	2.9	7.6

*Domestic shipments plus imports minus exports.

Source: Annual Statistical Report, American Iron and Steel Institute, 1980, Tables 1A and 1B, p. 8., 1981.

mand, the prevailing market price will be above the trigger price; the restriction will not be binding. During periods of slow economic growth, however, when steel mills in Japan are operating below 80 percent of capacity (used in the trigger-price formula), foreign producers would be willing to sell their steel in order to maximize their profits at below the trigger price. From a production point of view, foreign producers would be willing to increase output at the trigger price (Fig. 4.6).

Thus, the trigger price would be expected to have the following effects on the world market:

1. Since trigger prices operate as a minimum price, they are likely to become binding during periods of declining demand in a magnitude directly related to the slack in capacity. During periods of expansion, when plants are operating in excess of 80 percent capacity, they will be completely ineffective.

2. If effective, trigger prices would tend to reduce the demand for foreign steel and, thereby, its production. In a dynamic context, this implies that the U.S. market share of Japanese and European Economic Community steel production would decline. This is what happened between 1977 and 1980.

FIGURE 4.6.   The Effect of a Trigger Price on Output and Costs

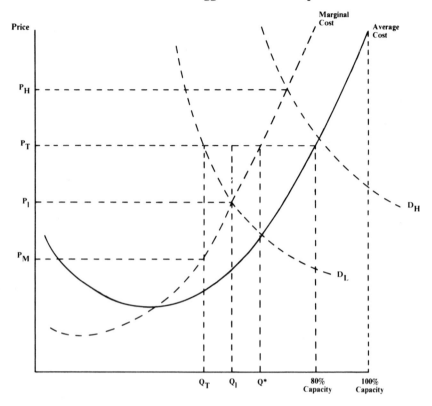

D_H	High level of demand
D_L	Low level of demand
Q_I	Quantity of foreign steel production without trigger prices when demand is low
Q_T	Quantity of foreign steel production with trigger prices
Q^*	Desired output of foreign steel producers with trigger price
P_I	Market price of steel when demand is low
P_H	Market price of steel when demand is high
P_T	Trigger price of steel
P_M	Marginal cost of production at the quantity of output with trigger prices (Q_T)
Q_I-Q_T	The reduction in foreign steel output due to trigger prices
P_T-P_M	The profit margin of foreign producers on increased production with trigger prices
$\left(\frac{P_T-P_I}{P_I}\right)$	Effective tax rate due to trigger prices that would produce similar quantity effects

3. The reduction in foreign steel market share will be satisfied by:

a. increased U.S. production;

b. increased foreign production from countries not covered by the trigger price agreements (non-Japanese, non-EEC). The distribution of the increase in production (among U.S. and rest-of-world producers) due to trigger prices depends on the shape of the U.S. and rest-of-world steel industry's cost curves;

c. increased price of steel in the U.S.

The data suggest that the adjustment to trigger prices incorporated all three of these factors.

4. The lower production level due to trigger prices results in a marginal cost of production substantially below the trigger prices and the full market price. In fact, quantity effects of the trigger price will be equivalent to a tax on the foreign steel imports (Fig. 4.6). Furthermore, to the extent that the trigger price increases the U.S. steel price, it will afford some effective protection to the industry.

5. The trigger price mechanism substantially increases profit margins for foreign producers. They are encouraged to bolster production even if the output is sold at below market prices or below trigger prices. This would happen since both prices would be above marginal costs. Incidences of dumping would be expected as a result. Thus, it is not surprising that the trigger price mechanism broke down after three years of slow U.S. and worldwide economic growth.

An important side effect of the trigger pricing mechanism was to protect European products from Japanese competition. To the extent Japanese steel prices were elevated by the trigger pricing agreement, European steelmakers were afforded the opportunity to garner market share they otherwise would have lost to less expensive Japanese steel.

The European cost disadvantage relative to actual Japanese production costs has remained. Viewed in this light, the subsidies to European mills are an effort to remain competitive with Japan in the all-important U.S. market. Through the subsidy, the marginal cost curve perceived by European producers is similar to the Japanese marginal cost curve.

In addition , the subsidy provides incentives for Europeans to sell steel in the U.S. below their home market or production costs—hence the charge of dumping.

The Steel Industry's Claim for Protection

The imposition of the current import quotas was the culmination of a legal process that began in January of 1982 when U.S. Steel and other domestic steel companies filed unfair trade practice petitions.[11] This spelled the end of the trigger pricing mechanism.

The plea for protection was prompted by compelling evidence that European and other governments were responding to the worldwide recession and overcapacity in steel by subsidizing producers in their own countries. At the same time, new steel-producing countries from the Third World, including Brazil and Romania, began penetrating the U.S. market. As a result, foreign steel was gaining U.S. market share even as total U.S. steel consumption was declining. During 1981, foreign steel increased its market share to 19.1 percent from 16.3 percent in 1980. On average, steel production in 1981 was slightly higher than in 1980 (Fig. 4.7). But the U.S. operating rate declined to 58.6 percent in December 1981 from 77.8 percent in the previous December. In response to this combination of falling output and eroding market share, the steel industry sought protection under the Trade Act of 1979.

Ironically, the steel industry's efforts to protect itself only aggravated its problems. Once the charges of unfair trade practices were filed, some foreign steelmakers increased their deliveries in an attempt to supply the U.S. before the Commerce Department's ruling, and hence, before the effective date for any duties or penalties. Between January and September of 1982, foreign steel shipments captured 24 percent of the U.S. market, and domestic operating rates declined to 39.8 percent, their lowest level since 1936.

Steel production also may have been adversely affected by industry efforts to curtail imports. The Standard and Poor's steel industry index fell relative to the S&P 500 when U.S. companies filed petitions in January and when the Commerce Department preliminarily upheld charges of subsidization and dumping in June. The relative value of the steel industry index remained unchanged when the final rulings announced lower subsidy rates, indicating lower duties. The performance of the steel industry index suggests that imposition of quotas also will be detrimental to the domestic steel industry. Whether or not a quota agreement would be reached in place of imposition of higher tariffs was not known until October 21. The steel industry index relative to the S&P 500 declined during October and remained unchanged the week following imposition of the quotas (Fig. 4.8).

The Trade Action Experience of 1982

U.S. Steel took the broadest action, filing countervailing duty petitions against producers in Belgium, France, Luxembourg, the Netherlands,

FIGURE 4.7. Steel Imports and U.S. Capability Utilization, 1975–July 1982

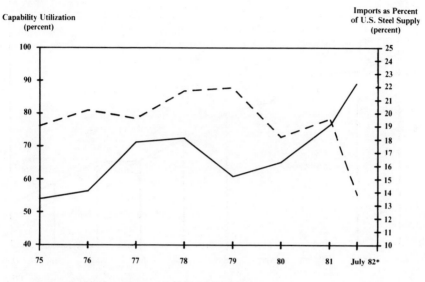

_____ Imports as percent of apparent U.S. steel supply
— — — U.S. raw steel capability utilization; average for period
*July 82 figure for imports is an average number from January through July 1982. July 82 figure for capability utilization is a year-to-date number based on weekly figures ending July 31, 1982.

Source: Annual Statistical Report, American Iron and Steel Institute, 1981.

the United Kingdom, West Germany, Brazil, South Africa and Spain. The first seven of these countries and Romania also were charged with dumping. Other actions were filed by Bethlehem Steel Corporation, LTV Corporations's Jones & Laughlin Steel Corporation, National Steel Corporation, Republic Steel Corporation, Inland Steel Corporation and Cyclops Corporation. Products covered by the filings are used in the auto, appliance and construction industries and represent about 70 percent of all carbon steel imports. U.S. Steel maintained that foreign governments were subsidizing these items ranging from $30 to $300 per ton and that dumping price margins ranged from $20 to $300 per ton.[12]

In its preliminary ruling, the Commerce Department found that nine foreign governments had been unfairly subsidizing steel exports. The International Trade Commission agreed that 90 percent of the unfair trade complaints represented reasonable injury to domestic steel products. The worse offender was the nationalized British Steel Corporation, which was found to be subsidizing 1981 exports by 40.4 percent of the average price

FIGURE 4.8. Steel Industry Index as a Percent of S&P 500

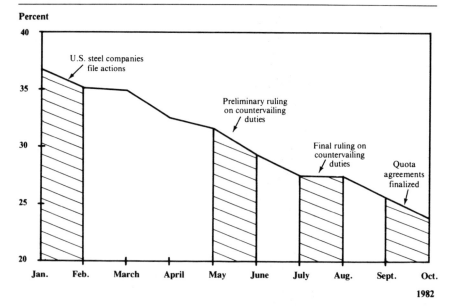

_____ Standard and Poor's Steel Industry Index divided by the Standard and Poor's 500 Index

Source: Standard and Poor's Current Statistics, S&P Corporation.

it charged in the U.S. Following British Steel were Société des Aciéries et Laminoirs de Lorraine in France by 30.0 percent, Cockerill Sambre in Belgium by 32.8 percent and Union Siderurgie du Nord et de l'Est de la France by 20.1 percent (Table 4.12).[13]

As a result of Commerce's preliminary ruling, steel importers were required to post cash or bonds on products coming from the cited companies to cover penalty duties that may be imposed later. The department also decided, for the first time, to make some penalties retroactive. Some imports from Belgium and France would be assessed retroactive penalties for 90 days because of a "surge of shipments apparently intended to beat the statutory deadlines for imposition of anti-dumping duties" (Table 4.13).[14]

The Commerce Department's final ruling reduced most of the subsidy margins cited in its preliminary determinations and narrowed the list of offenders to six Western European countries. The estimated subsidy for the British Steel Corporation, for example, was cut to 20 percent— half the level of the preliminary finding. The cases against Brazil and the

TABLE 4.12. Commerce Department Rulings on Subsidization: Countervailing Duty Determinations

Country	Company		Net Subsidy Ad Valorem Rate*	
			Preliminary Ruling June 17	*Final Ruling September 7*
Belgium	Fabrique de Fer de Charleroi	min	1.990	2.165
	Siderurgie Maritime		4.866	2.771
	Cockerill Sambre	max	20.602–21.773	13.225–13.411
Brazil	Companhia Siderurgica Paulista		8.580	Case dropped
	Usinas Siderurgicas de Minas Gerais S.A.		8.580	
France	Société Anonyme des Forges et des Aciéries de Dilling	min	—	3.702–4.038
	Union Siderurgie du Nord et de l'Est de la France		20.097	11.300–17.980
	Société des Aciéries et des Laminoirs de Lorraine	max	30.029	11.300–21.416
Germany	AG der Dillinge Huttenwerke	min	0.551	**
	Stahlwerke Rochling— Burbach GmbH	max	8.623	1.131
Italy	A.F.L. Falck. S.p.A.	min	18.30	6.32
	Nuova Italsider, S.p.A.	max	18.30	14.56

TABLE 4.12. (continued)

Luxembourg	Aciéries Réunies de Burbach–Eich–Dudelange S.A.		1.766	min	0.539
	Metallurgique et Minière de Rodange—Athus S.A.		1.766	max	1.523
Netherlands	Estel Hoogovens B.V.		0.651		Case dropped
South Africa	Highveld Steel and Vanadium Corporation		7.8–8.0		12.1***
	South African Iron and Steel Industrial Corporation		6.4–10.2		6.7–15.1***
U.K.	Flather Bright Steel, Ltd.	min	2.445	min	****
	Brymbo Steel Works, Ltd.		—		1.880
	British Steel Corporation	max	40.362	max	20.330

*Based on net subsidy for each firm within each country.

**Estimated net subsidy was found to be de minimis and therefore not subject to duty.

***For products exported before April 1, 1982, and entered or withdrawn from warehouse on or after September 7; products exported on or after April 1, 1982, no duty applies.

****Excluded from determinations.

Note: Companies investigated include only those cited in the petitions filed by U.S. companies.

Source: "Preliminary Affirmative Countervailing Duty Determinations," *Federal Register*, Department of Commerce, International Trade Administration, June 17, 1982; "Final Affirmative Countervailing Duty Determinations," *Federal Register*, Department of Commerce, International Trade Administration, September 7, 1982.

TABLE 4.13. Imports of Steel from France and Belgium

1982	Steel Sheets		Steel Plates		Total Structural Shapes	
	Belgium	France	Belgium	France	Belgium	France
Jan.	6.027	23.629	19.895	6.086	31.078	2.776
Feb.	863	19.782	17.808	6.282	26.258	609
March	1.879	8.846	22.819	4.208	13.421	1.400
April	2.395	779	15.179	719	13.990	3.265
May	12.225	11.652	19.201	3.186	27.786	7.575
June	11.241	34.034	40.061	15.840	48.850	10.926
July	12.000	6.027	16.914	3.940	30.828	1.350

Source: American Iron and Steel Institute.

Netherlands were dropped. The subsidy findings for South Africa were reduced from a high of 16.3 percent to less than 1 percent, eliminating penalty actions against this country, as well. (Table 4.12).[15]

Toward the end of the summer, the Commerce Department also found that carbon steel from Belgium, Germany, France, Italy, the United Kingdom and Romania was being dumped on the U.S. market. Of imports in 1981, Teksid in Italy was found to have the greatest dumping margin, pricing cold-rolled sheet and strip products 40.7 percent below the cost of production. British Steel Corporation, in addition to having the greatest subsidy margin, was found also to have dumping margins of 18.8 percent on steel plate and 10.6 on structural steel (Table 4.14).[15]

On October 21, just hours before the Commerce Department would have been required to impose countervailing and penalty duties, quota negotiations were finalized, limiting European steel imports to about 85 percent of 1981 levels. In addition, the quotas were extended to pipe and tube products. The accord had two parts:[16]

1. Carbon and alloy steel shipments were limited to an average 5.44 percent of the projected U.S. market. The pact also set individual ceilings for specific categories (Table 4.15). The Europeans were directed to set up a new export licensing system to enforce this part of the accord.

2. Pipe and tube exports were restricted to 5.9 percent of expected U.S. demand. If this limit seemed likely to be breached, the two sides would have 60 days to find a settlement. Otherwise, either could impose new restrictions.

TABLE 4.14. Dumping Margins (Weighted Average Margin in Percent)

Type of Product	Belgium	West Germany	France	Italy	Luxem.	Nether.	Romania	U.K.
Carbon steel structural shapes	1.14	4.94	9.06	—	0.46*	—	—	10.61
Hot-rolled carbon steel plate	1.88	8.22	—	—	—	—	13.2	18.84
Hot-rolled carbon steel sheet and strip	9.83	3.94	8.40	2.07	—	0.003*	—	—
Cold-rolled carbon steel sheet and strip	—	6.43	11.50	9.72	—	0.37*	—	—

Dumping Margin Range by Company

Country		Company	Weighted Average Margin** in Percent
Belgium	Max	Cockerill Sambre	10.88

	Min	Fabrique de Fer de Charleroi	0.79
Germany	Max	Thyssen AG	19.17
	Min	Klockner-Werke AG	0.65
France	Max	Société des Aciéries et des Laminoirs de Lorraine	27.69
	Min	Société Anonyme des Forges et des Aciéries de Dilling	0.19
Italy	Max	Teksid S.p.A.	40.78
	Min	Nuova Italsider S.p.A.	2.07
Romania		Metalimportexport	13.20 (one single rate)
U.K.	Max	British Steel Corporation	18.84
	Min	Darlington-Simpson Rolling Mills	7.84

*The weighted average margin on all sales is de minimis, or not being or likely to be sold at less than fair value.

**The Customs Service requires a cash deposit or the posting of a bond equal to the estimated weighted average margin by which the foreign market value of the merchandise subject to these investigations exceeds the U.S. price.

Source: Federal Register: "Preliminary Determination of Sales at Less Than Fair Value," August 16, 1982, Department of Commerce, International Trade Administration.

TABLE 4.15. Quotas by Type of Steel in Percent of Projected U.S. Market

Type of Steel	Percent	Type of Steel	Percent
Sheet piling	21.85	Cold-rolled sheet	5.11
Structurals	9.91	Wire-rod	4.29
Rail	8.9	Oated sheet	3.27
Hot-rolled sheet and strip	6.81	Hot-rolled bars	2.38
Plate	5.36	Tin plate	2.2

Source: Wall Street Journal.

In an effort to enforce the agreement, the U.S. invoked a newly enacted law allowing the Customs Service to block specified steel imports without foreign export licenses.

Taking each European country in isolation, quotas promise to offset the advantages of any subsidy. Experience with Voluntary Restraint Agreements and trigger pricing, however, dramatizes that foreign producers cannot be taken in isolation. Although the quotas were successful in reducing the amount of EEC and Japanese steel into the U.S., it is not at all clear that the U.S. producers took advantage of these opportunities. In fact, the data suggest that the void left by the EEC steel was quickly filled by Canadian and Latin American producers (Tables 4.10, 4.11). In fact, from 1982 to 1983, Latin America more than doubled its exports to the U.S., increasing its share of the U.S. market to a respectable 2.9 percent.

Seeking A Global Solution

Using a global approach yields a much different answer. The following market responses would be expected to work to eliminate protection offered by the quotas:

Trade patterns would change. The world supply of steel would tend to move around the new quotas much as water moves around an obstacle that only partially blocks a river. The flow of the water is distorted at the point of interference, but little is changed downstream.

For example, European steelmakers who face quotas would become less competitive in the U.S. But they would try to maintain production by increasing shipments of steel to non-U.S. markets where they also compete with Japanese, Koreans, South Africans and other world class steelmakers. At the same time, these foreign producers would be facing stiffer competition in non-U.S. markets, but they would be facing less competition in the U.S. market due to the decrease in European imports. Hence, they would tend to increase their shipments to the U.S., competing with domestic producers for the market share lost by the Europeans.

This analysis is supported by the world market response to trigger prices. In their aftermath, the decline in Japanese and European market share was almost totally offset by other foreign producers. Initial market responses also were consistent with this analysis. In August, imports from Japan were up 48 percent from their July level while imports from the Common Market were down 7.8 percent as U.S. customers of foreign steel reportedly began to hedge against barriers to European imports.[17] All told, steel imports were up 30 percent in August relative to July levels.

The product mix would change. The product mix shift which occurred during the 1969–74 import quota period can be expected to be repeated. Unlike the VRAs, the newly imposed quotas are on an item by item basis. This approach would limit the shift to higher-valued steel imports that occurred under the VRAs. But not all European steel is covered; the notable exception is specialty steels. Thus, European steelmakers would be expected to increase shipments of the high-valued product to the U.S. market.

The form of steel would change. Quotas are imposed on raw steel only. Thus, market forces would create incentives to partially fabricate or finish the steel before it is shipped to the U.S. Likewise, American consumers would have an incentive to purchase less expensive foreign steel in fabricated form. For example, foreign mills might ship the raw steel formerly destined for the U.S. market to steel service centers located in Canada. Once fabricated, the steel would be exported to end users in the U.S. Or, American consumers may simply obtain the steel in finished form by purchasing more foreign steel. Since these products would be made with the low-priced foreign steel, their price also would tend to be lower relative to goods produced in the U.S. from higher-priced domestic steel.

The choice of a quota versus a tariff is important to three groups in particular: domestic importers, foreign exporters and the government. Under a tariff, all revenue from the wedge imposed on imports accrues to the government. However, under a quota, the equivalent revenue could accrue to any one of the three groups, depending upon how the quota is administered. For example, if rights to import the limited quantities are given to domestic importers, this group receives benefits from the restriction. In this case, the importer buys the protected goods at the world price, yet sells the goods at the same higher price as the domestic producers. The difference in price is additional revenue for the importer. Thus, a quota represents more profit to the importer than does the equivalent tariff.

Alternatively, the U.S. could instruct the foreign country simply to limit its exports to the U.S. In this case, foreigners must decide how to distribute the limited rights to sell goods in the U.S. Those fortunate foreigners who receive these rights reap benefits from the export quota. Since foreigners receive the benefits, this case is equivalent to foreigners imposing tariffs on the U.S.

Finally, the United States government could choose to implement the quota by auctioning off import rights to the highest bidder. Competition for the import rights would then drive down the net profits of domestic importers or foreign exporters until they were the same as in the absence of the quota. The government's total revenues from this policy should be approximately equal to the revenues from imposing the equivalent tariff.[18]

The current quota agreement extends the government-sanctioned steel cartel now operating in Europe to the U.S. market. Any changes in the competitive position among European steelmakers will not be reflected in the U.S. market without government approval. The U.S. market will tend to ossify.

The increasing pressures to finish the cartelization of the domestic market by imposing quotas on all other foreign suppliers testifies as perhaps no other event to the failure of trade protectionism to improve the vitality of the domestic steel industry.

Early in 1984, countervailing duties against Argentina, Brazil and Mexico were sought. The petition against Mexico subsequently was dropped when that country agreed to year-long, renewable export quotas on certain steel products. By summer, the Commerce Department had published affirmative subsidy determinations against Brazil and Argentina. In the case of Argentina, the finding was final; Brazil was awaiting a final "injury test" determination by the ITC. New petitions involving the dumping of oil-country tubular goods were filed against five countries—Mexico, Argentina, Brazil, Spain and South Korea—and were to be acted on by the Commerce Department in July.[19]

In summary, the imposition of quotas on selected foreign steel suppliers:

• Will not increase significantly domestic steelmaker's market share, profitability, employment or investment.

- Will decrease the U.S. market share held by France, Britain, Italy and other countries facing quotas.
- Will increase the U.S. market share captured by Japan, Korea, and other countries that do not face quotas. U.S. steelmakers will share disproportionately less in this gain because of the significant advantages in economy of scale operations enjoyed by foreign competitors.
- Will increase foreign competition for U.S. steel service centers and fabricators.
- Will increase foreign competition for domestic industries intensive in the use of steel, including autos, appliances, and oil and gas.
- Will leave world steel production nearly unchanged.
- Will decrease only slightly the efficiency of the world economy.

Extension of these quotas to all foreign suppliers of a fixed share of the U.S. market will:

- Increase the domestic steelmaker's market share.
- Lead to circumvention through increased imports of foreign steel in semifabricated or fabricated form.
  —Imports of products with a large steel content, from appliances to machine tools and autos, will increase.
  —Absent restrictions, profitability and employment of these industries will tend to decline. Based on the empirical analysis reported earlier in Case II, this deterioration will lead to protectionist pressure in these newly "injured" industries.
- This circumvention implies that the degree of protection afforded by expanding the steel quotas will be far less than assumed.
  —The domestic industry's shipments and employment will not increase as much as implied by the enforced increase in market share because the size of the U.S. steel market will shrink.

CASE III: THE AUTOMOBILE INDUSTRY

In May 1981, U.S. trade negotiators were successful in securing a "voluntary" export restraint by Japanese automobile manufacturers to limit their U.S. exports to 1.68 million units for the year ending May 1, 1982. That agreement allowed the second-year export figure to exceed the 1.68 million mark by 16.5 percent of the growth in U.S. auto sales. For the third year, exports to the U.S. are monitored on a monthly basis as stated by the Foreign Exchange and Foreign Trade Control Law.

The call for protection from Japanese imports came after a tumultuous decade for the domestic auto industry. The oil embargo and subsequent inflation in 1973–74 had a major impact on the U.S. economy generally, but the disruption was felt even more severely in the automobile industry.

Prior to the 1974–75 recession and fourfold jump in oil prices, unit sales of domestic automakers had increased on a steady basis to 9.67 million in 1973. In 1974, sales dropped 2.2 million units, or 23 percent. Sales began to pick up in 1976, and were just slightly below their 1973 peak when the overthrow of the Shah of Iran occurred in 1979. This led to a second rapid increase in gasoline prices and uncertain product availability. Once again, auto sales plummeted. By 1982, U.S. new car sales had declined to 5.8 million units, their lowest point since 1961.

Market Composition: Small vs. Large Cars

During this period of a shrinking market, there was a dramatic change in the composition of automobile sales in the U.S. Three factors in particular contributed to this change: the slow-down in economic growth, the increase in federal regulations and the rise in the real price of gasoline.

From the peak sales year of 1973 until 1982, full-size car sales declined, losing more than 15 percent of market share (Fig. 4.9a). The change in market share of intermediate autos was much less dramatic than that of either small- or full-size cars. Between 1973 and 1980, sales declined by just 322,000 units (Fig. 4.9b) and market share declined only 2.6 percentage points. During the 1973–80 period, sales of small cars in the U.S. increased by 1.1 million units. In the face of declining overall automobile sales, this enabled the small car share of market to increase by more than 20 percent, to 63.8 percent in 1980 from 42.7 percent in 1973. In 1979, one year after the peak in general auto sales, small car sales reached their high of 6.0 million units.

Market Composition: Foreign vs. Domestic Cars

More than 97 percent of all imported cars are within the small car market, and 89 percent of all imports are subcompacts. As a result, the change in the past decade in the composition of the U.S. auto market toward small cars sustained foreign car sales even though total U.S. auto sales were declining. During the first eight years, import share ranged

FIGURE 4.9. The Changing Composition of the U.S. Auto Market by Car Size, 1970–83

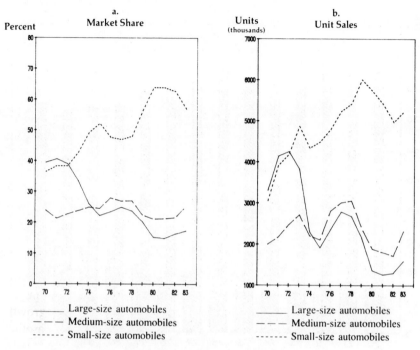

a.
Percent Market Share

b.
Units
(thousands) Unit Sales

——— Large-size automobiles
— — — Medium-size automobiles
------- Small-size automobiles

——— Large-size automobiles
— — — Medium-size automobiles
------- Small-size automobiles

Source: Ward's Data Bank; *Wall Street Journal.*

between 14.5 percent and 18.5 percent (Fig. 4.10). In 1979, import penetration increased, climbing to a peak of 27.8 percent in 1982.

An examination of the overall market indicates that the U.S. loss in market share was not due to a sudden or unusual increase in the competitive position of Japanese or other foreign car makers. Rather, it was a result of the change in composition of the market. The subcompact share of the U.S. auto market increased to 43 percent in 1981 from 24 percent in 1971. During this time, foreign car makers maintained a stable portion of the subcompact market, leading inexorably to an increase in their overall market share.

The Importance of the Voluntary Restraint Agreements

In 1983, the Japanese share of the market slipped to 20.9 percent from its year earlier 22.7 percent. In addition, U.S. producers increased their

FIGURE 4.10.   Share of the Total U.S. Market, Domestic and Imported Autos

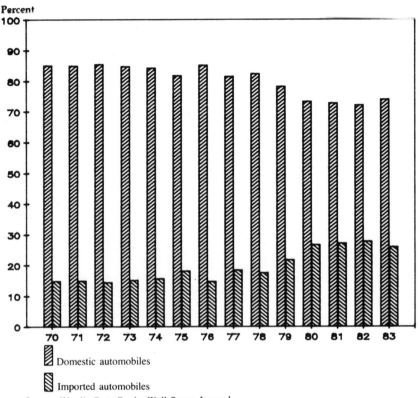

Source: Ward's Data Bank; *Wall Street Journal.*

market share to 50 percent in 1983 from 46 percent in 1981. This could be interpreted as evidence that the restraints on Japanese auto imports have in fact worked. However, a closer look at the data suggests that these results cannot be solely attributed to the restrictions.

If the VRAs had caused the decline in Japanese auto imports, and European cars were substitutes for Japanese cars, one would have expected to see Europeans picking up part of the slack. However, during this period, European car imports declined as well. In addition, the number of European units sold has declined, even though these cars are not subject to the VRAs, while Japanese car sales have actually increased (Table 4.16).

The decline in the Japanese market share can more properly be at-

**TABLE 4.16. Domestic and Imported Automobiles,
Units Sold and Market Share**

Market Segment	1979	1980	1981	1982	1983
Total Units Sold Domestic and Import	10,517,203	8,931,607	8,475,395	7,938,159	9,149,261
Domestic	8,212,681	6,546,634	6,162,275	5,756,660	6,795,302
Percent of Market	78.6	73.3	72.8	72.5	74.4
Import	2,253,588	2,384,973	2,313,120	2,181,499	2,353,959
Percent of Market	21.4	26.7	27.2	27.5	25.6
Japanese	1,755,968	1,908,423	1,858,913	1,801,969	1,917,621
Percent of Market	16.7	21.4	21.9	22.7	20.9
European	497,620	476,550	454,207	379,530	436,338
Percent of Market	4.7	5.3	5.3	4.8	4.7

Source: Wall Street Journal.

tributed to the 23 percent decline in the price of gasoline and the economic recovery. As a result of these factors, the market share of small cars declined 6.9 percentage points to 56.9 percent in 1983 from 63.8 percent in 1981. The Japanese, which almost exclusively produce small cars, lost market share with the decline in the small car market.

Although the import quotas negotiated with the Japanese have done little to alleviate the auto industry's problems, it is likely that these trade restrictions have impaired the domestic industry's long-run competitive position. Due to import restrictions, the domestic industry has increased its capacity to produce small, low-profit-margin cars. Symmetrically, the restraints have forced the Japanese to emphasize more than they otherwise would have the larger, more profitable segments of their production. This "upward filtering" is the inevitable result of quantity restrictions. For any given level of total profit, a company can choose between selling a large number of low-margin items or a smaller number of high-margin items. In the case of automobiles, the higher the value of the car, generally the higher will be the absolute per car margin. When a ceiling is placed on the number of units which can be sold, the rational response by sellers is to fill that quota with high-priced items. Hence, the effect of a quota is to upgrade the entire product mix, supplying more high-priced cars and fewer low-priced models than in the absence of a quota.

For example, Japanese auto dealers in the U.S. would be expected to "load" the models they do receive with more expensive, previously optional equipment. The implicit burden of the quantity restriction would be lower as a percentage of a "loaded" auto than of a "stripped-down" model. Accordingly, as the constraint becomes more tightly binding, one would expect to see only fully equipped autos being offered by Japanese import dealers. Any options which can be added by the dealer, such as "top of the line" radios, air conditioners and trim packages, would become non-optional extras at additional cost.

The quality response to quantity import restrictions was evident in the U.S. experience with steel import restrictions similar to those now being imposed on Japanese autos.[20] In the case of steel, even though the quantity of imports was reduced, the value of total imports actually increased. Moreover, the profitability of the steel industry during the period of the voluntary restraints was lower than it was in the unrestricted periods three years before and two years after. A similar quality response to a quantity restriction also was evident in the case of nonrubber footwear.[21]

Indeed, this effect was immediately evident in the U.S. auto market. Commerce Department figures show that from April through September of 1981, the first six months of import controls, Japanese auto imports declined 12.4 percent relative to the year earlier. But the value of these imports increased by 23 percent, far more than can be explained by inflation. During this period, the average sticker price of each car rose 28.7 percent to $5,324.[22] In the next two years, the increase was even greater. The average sticker price jumped by $2,600, a rise of 35 percent from April 1981 to March 1983. According to Wharton Econometric Forecasting Associates, as much as $1,000 of that can be attributed to the impact of the voluntary restrictions.[23]

Ironically, if the upgrading hypothesis proves correct, the VRA may prove to be responsible for conferring considerable benefit on Japanese auto makers in the coming decade. If real gasoline prices continue the decline triggered by U.S. decontrol of oil prices,[24] the future of small, fuel-efficient automobiles may not be as bright as many are forecasting. While Detroit has undergone a major retooling shift toward compact and subcompact production capacity, Japan is being encouraged by the VRA to shift toward relatively larger, less fuel-efficient and more luxurious cars.

In addition, market forces have prompted efforts to circumvent the VRAs. One strategy is to build new plants outside of Japan that can produce small cars for the U.S. market. Toyota, for example, is planning to locate an auto production facility in Taiwan that will be able to export to the U.S. as well as Southeast Asia. Domestic automakers are pursuing similar strategies. Ford has announced its intention to build a small-car plant in Mexico, and GM plans to enter into a joint venture in Korea to build small cars that can be exported to the U.S. market. Not coincidentally, these countries, Taiwan, Mexico and Korea, are the exact same countries where color TV manufacturing moved when VRAs were imposed on Japanese color TVs.[25]

Subsequently, the U.S. broadened the coverage of VRAs to these countries as well. The industry response was to establish plants in the U.S. that had a minimal value added, but effectively circumvented the import restrictions.[26]

Toyota and Honda have also moved to circumvent the VRAs by establishing manufacturing facilities in the U.S.: Toyota, through its joint venture with GM, and Honda, through its solely owned manufacturing facilities in Ohio.

Because of these moves, the degree of protection afforded domestic automakers by the VRAs is far less than it appears and is diminishing rapidly. Allowing the VRAs to lapse would not be expected to adversely affect the market values of the domestic auto companies.

The Threat of Local Content Laws

In 1982, Douglas Fraser, president of the United Auto Workers, began to lobby for a strict "North American content" law. In general, the greater the sales of cars in the U.S. market, the greater the percentage of the value added of a car to be produced in North America (Table 4.17).

By their very design, local content laws would be quite restrictive on imports of the high-volume, small cars produced by Japan while exempting the lower-volume, large cars produced by Europe. Thus, Toyotas and Nissans and other cars serving the broad middle class would be restricted while the availability of Mercedes and BMWs enjoyed by high income earners would be left largely unaffected.

U.S. automakers also could be affected adversely by local content laws. Their ability to expand sourcing of components such as small engines from their foreign plants and foreign suppliers would be curtailed. And foreign-owned automotive plants already in the U.S. such as Volkswagen's and Honda's car plants and Nissan's light truck plant, likely would be shut down by the law. Car prices in the U.S. would rise, car sales would decline and standards of living would fall.

Market forces also would be unleashed that could change the structure of the auto industry worldwide. The exemption of the low-volume companies from the local content legislation would create enormous in-

TABLE 4.17. Domestic Content Requirements for Motor Vehicles proposed in H.R. 5133

Number of vehicles sold by manufacturer during such year	Local Content Required (percent)		
	1983	1984	1985
Less than 100,000	0	0	0
Over 100,000 but less than 150,000	8.3	16.7	25.0
Over 150,000 but less than 200,000	16.7	33.3	50.0
Over 200,000 but less than 500,000	25.0	50.0	75.0
Over 500,000	30.0	60.0	90.0

Source: H.R. 5133, House of Representatives, 9th Congress (1981).

centives to fragment the auto industry. Ford and GM, for example, would have an incentive to transform their foreign subsidiaries into independent companies, each able to export to the U.S. under the local content umbrella. At first, smaller Japanese automakers would expand their market share at the expense of their larger competitors. But the larger Japanese automakers, too, could be expected to seek to circumvent the restrictions by creating new, smaller competitors in the newly industrialized countries from Taiwan and Korea to Brazil.

All of this analysis, of course, ignores the international repercussions of such restrictionist policies in the U.S. Automakers in Europe and Canada, in particular, could be expected to face an enormous increase in competition from the Japanese cars diverted from the U.S. market. Thus, a rolling pattern of increased trade restrictions could easily engulf the world economy. It should never be forgotten that the Smoot–Hawley Tariff began as an effort to protect the American farmer from cheap, foreign competition and ended with the misery and poverty so vividly captured in the *Grapes of Wrath*.

In any case, imposition of local content laws would be expected to impair the long-run profitability of the domestic auto industry and depress the equity values of the protected companies.

CASE IV: THE U.S. EXPORT EMBARGO ON SUPERPHOSPHORIC ACID

In the aftermath of the Soviet Union's invasion of Afghanistan, the U.S. embargoed the export of grain, superphosphoric acid and other assorted products to the Soviet Union. The ostensible purpose was to damage the Soviet economy by increasing the cost of several of its major imports. The embargo was lifted on April 24, 1981.

The U.S. has a superior technology in the production of super-phosphoric acid (SPA), a high grade industrial material, with near sub-stitutes being available elsewhere in the world. However, the capital em-ployed in the production of SPA could not be used economically to produce other lower grade, phosphoric acid-based products. For all in-tents and purposes, the capital was immobile.

The embargo of the export of superphosphoric acid to the Soviet Un-ion contains elements of both Scenario II, "A World With Factor Mo-bility Only within National Boundaries," and Scenario III, "A World in Which Capital is Immobile Across Industries and/or Countries," dis-cussed in Chapter 3.

The impact of the embargo on the Soviet Union is to a large extent analogous to Scenario II. The supplies of a commodity (in this case, su-perphosphoric acid) were cut off by the U.S. But there were other coun-tries in the rest of the world capable of supplying close substitutes for the embargoed commodity. Under this scerario, when the source of supplies from one country is interrupted or restricted, the gap is filled by supplies from the rest of the world.

The impact of the embargo on the U.S., however, is represented by Scenario III. In this scenario, the rate of return in the exporting country on capital and labor employed in the production of the embargoed com-modity falls. The more immobile the capital, the lower will be its rate of return. At the same time, the rate of return on capital in the produc-tion of the embargoed material in the importing country rises, inducing the importing country to employ more capital and labor in that industry. Since the importing country is asumed to have an inferior technology, it may import technological capabilities (plan design and construction) as well.

Effects of the SPA Embargo

The embargo of a highly concentrated fertilizer, a superphosphoric acid (SPA) to the Soviet Union, provides an example that dramatizes many of the double-edged effects of trade restrictions in general and embargoes against the Soviet Union in particular. The apparent ability of this em-bargo to harm the Soviet economy seemed high. SPA was produced by Occidental Petroleum Company using a unique process. Unlike the grain embargo, no perfect substitute analogous to Canadian wheat existed.

Nonetheless, the Soviet Union was able to obtain other phosphoric acid products under long-term contracts from companies in Belgium, Morocco, Tunisia and South Africa. The use of these substitutes imposed relatively small incremental costs on the Soviet production process. By contrast, the costs to American citizens were quite consequential. Output and jobs were transferred to foreign countries. Occidental, which had built its plant under a long-term contract with the Soviet Union, suffered substantial losses.

In order for the U.S. embargo of SPA exports to the Soviet Union to have been successful, the rest of the world had to cooperate with the U.S. by not providing alternative supplies to the Soviet Union. However, the evidence suggests that this cooperation was not forthcoming. Europeans, in general, are much more reluctant than the U.S. to use trade as a political weapon. As a result, Soviet trade with Western Europeans has risen sharply in the aftermath of U.S. trade restraints following the Russian invasion of Afghanistan.

Patterns of Trade: Alternative Sources

Phosphoric acid (P_2O_5) is available in various forms that differ in their concentration and purity. Superphosphoric acid is the highest form commercially available, which makes it especially valuable as a basic raw material for the production of fertilizers and other phosphoric acid-based products. However, the substitution of other phosphoric acid products for SPA induces relatively small incremental costs in the Soviet production process. The Soviet Union has been able to obtain such alternate supplies of phosphoric acid. During 1981, the Soviets secured phosphoric acid from, among others, Morocco, India, Japan, Mexico and Turkey.

The Soviets did not begin immediately to replace the U.S.-embargoed phosphates. Apparently, they either hoped that the U.S. embargo would be short-term or they realized that phosphoric acid could not be shipped in time for spring application. In April 1979, however, the Soviets began to make inquiries about obtaining additional sources of phosphoric acid.

The Soviet–Moroccan trade negotiations culminated in November 1980, with a 30-year agreement which included the signing of a protocol on the exchange of Soviet nitrogen and potash fertilizers and some other goods for the Moroccan phosphoric acid and triple superphosphate in the period from 1981 to 1985.[27]

In addition, the Belgian company Lste. Industrielle de Prayons, in association with its subsidiary Chemie Rupel, has agreed to supply

100,000–150,000 t.p.a. of concentrated phosphoric acid to the U.S.S.R. for five years starting in April 1981. The acid is most likely 65 to 68 percent P_2O_5. Prayons is one of the few volume producers of purified phosphoric acid in West Europe, having a capacity 90,000 t.p.a. P_2O_5.[28]

Phosphoric acid also was available to the Soviet Union from India (1,082,000 metric tons projected for 1981), Japan (717,000 metric tons projected for 1981), Mexico (611,000 metric tons projected for 1981), and Turkey (530,000 metric tons projected for 1981).[29]

By the spring of 1981, the Soviets were able to replace almost half of the 700,000 tons of phosphoric acid that would have been exported as superphosphoric acid by the United States if the embargo had not been imposed. They were prepared to use, and had contracted for, supplies of merchant grade phosphoric acid, diammonium phosphate (DAP), and triple superphosphate (TSP) to replace the P_2O_5 equivalent of the embargoed SPA (Table 4.18).[30]

Several of the tonnages listed in Table 4.18 are part of larger, long-term contracts with the Soviet Union, discussed in earlier paragraphs, which assure the Soviet Union a steady source of phosphate from these countries.

Finally, the Soviet Union is the second largest producer of fertilizer nutrients and phosphates in the world. Furthermore, they have had significant excess P_2O_5 capacity available. Over the past five years, production has exceeded domestic consumption by substantial amounts.[31]

As a result of these factors, the embargo did not and could not serve to deprive the Soviet Union of phosphate fertilizer. On the contrary, it merely shifted the export business from U.S. suppliers to their competitors.

TABLE 4.18. Replacement Supplies of Phosphoric Acid Obtained by the Soviet Union

Supplier	Tonnage (metric tons)	Source of Information
Morocco (OCP)	29,000	British sulphur
	10,000	Fertecon monthly report
	41,000	Fertecon monthly report
Belgium (Prayons)	70,000	Fertecon monthly report
South Africa	70–80,000	British sulphur
Tunisia (ICM)	22,000	British sulphur
Total	252,000	

The Soviets also were in a position to acquire the technology to produce concentrated, if not superphosphoric, acid. Rhone-Poulenc, S.A., and the Soviet Union in November 1976 concluded a ten year trade agreement that would furnish the Russians with agricultural products, animal feed, agrochemical factories and know-how in exchange for shipments of chemicals and raw materials. Estimates of the ten year pact's total value range from $6.5 billion to $8.6 billion.

Under this pact, Rhone-Poulenc signed a contract worth six billion francs to provide the Soviets with three fertilizer plants, a phosphate acid facility, two plants producing crop protection products, and a methanol unit.

In addition, the Soviets negotiated with the French contractor, PEC Engineering, to purchase "concentration units" which would enable the Russians to import merchant trade phosphoric acid and produce their own SPA. PEC Engineering previously had sold the Russians seven liquid fertilizer plants.

Impact on U.S. Producers

The phosphate tonnage diverted by reason of the U.S. embargo caused temporary oversupply, temporary price depression, and disruption of trading patterns in domestic and, to a lesser extent, in world phosphate markets, as the economies and trade adjusted to the embargo. The domestic phosphate fertilizer industry lost substantial revenue due to the embargo, because domestic producers were forced to shift production to lower grade phosphates, and to modify plant facilities, terminals and ships which were specifically designed and built for the production of high-grade phosphoric acid.

For example, since the imposition of the embargo, Occidental Petroleum Company has produced more merchant acid than any other phosphate product. Occidental has exported most of this merchant acid to Brazil, Indonesia, Mexico and Turkey. These exports caused temporary oversupply and price declines in world markets.

The embargo also forced Occidental to change totally its production plans, modify its plant facilities, terminals and ships to accommodate the altered production plans, and seek contracts and arrange for shipment of the new mix of phosphoric fertilizers. Occidental estimates that the loss in profits resulting from these extensive changes will be in the tens of millions of dollars.

The most significant portion of this loss is attributable to the much lower profit margins Occidental has realized from its sales of merchant acid and DAP than it could have realized from its SPA sales. Profit margins were significantly lower for two reasons. First, SPA, a higher quality product than either merchant acid or DAP, commands a much higher price. Second, because of the oversupply of phosphoric acid, merchant acid and DAP prices have been depressed.

Moreover, Occidental is incurring high merchant acid production costs, because its SPA facility was not designed to produce merchant acid. In order to adjust quickly to the phosphate embargo, Occidental had to utilize its present SPA facilities to produce the merchant grade P_2O_5. While this conversion required only relatively minor adjustments to the SPA facilities, use of this facility for merchant acid production is expensive and inefficient, since it purifies the acid to a degree not required in conventional merchant acid production. In effect, the capital employed in the production of SPA was highly immobile.

This combination of relatively high production costs and greatly reduced selling prices resulted in a dramatic reduction in Occidental's phosphate profits in 1980. The reduction in profits has a particularly acute impact in the company's fertilizer operations, because of the substantial investment—$450 million—in the White Springs, Florida facilities. Occidental made this investment to modify and expand existing phosphate operations and to construct additional facilities in order to fulfill its obligations under its agreement to supply SPA to the U.S.S.R.

Finally, while the point at which the Soviets finally decided to abrogate their 20-year contract agreement with Occidental was uncertain, it is clear that the longer the phosphate embargo continued, the more the entire agreement was jeopardized. In the months before the embargo was lifted, two events indicated that the Russians' patience was waning. First, the Soviets periodically threatened to reduce or terminate ammonia, urea and potash shipments to the U.S. and hence, to Occidental. The stated reason for these threats was the U.S. embargo of SPA shipments to the Soviet Union. Second, the Soviets had begun to discuss with other countries the construction of SPA plants. These discussions clearly suggested that the Soviets were seeking an alternative, reliable supplier of SPA to replace the U.S.

Moreover, even as the embargo was lifted, the securing of alternative sources by the Russians implied that Occidental had to commit itself to long-term production of merchant acid and granular fertilizers. This required substantial additional investment to convert the SPA facility to a conventional merchant acid facility with competitive production costs.

This analysis suggests that the embargo had a negative impact on the market price of Occidental Petroleum stock. In an efficient market where prices reflect public information about Occidental, one would expect a correlation between the announcement of the embargo and the decline in the market price of the stock.

In the aftermath of the embargo, the price of Occidental Petroleum and the stock market index (Standard and Poor's 500) declined (Fig. 4.11). One possible interpretation of the decline in the Standard and Poor's 500 is that the embargo imposed by President Carter had economy-wide effects. The price of Occidental stock, however, declined even more than the Standard and Poor's 500 (Fig. 4.12). This result is consistent with the view that the embargo had a greater effect on Occidental than on the rest of the economy.

FIGURE 4.11. The Trade Weapon and the Stock Market

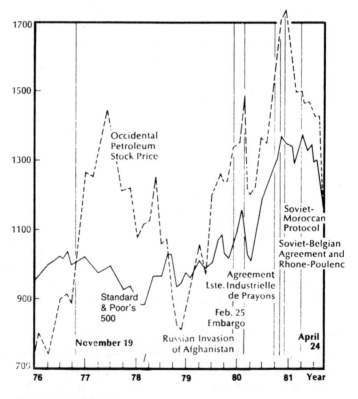

Source: Occidental Petroleum Co.

FIGURE 4.12.   Impact of the SPA Embargo on Occidental Petroleum

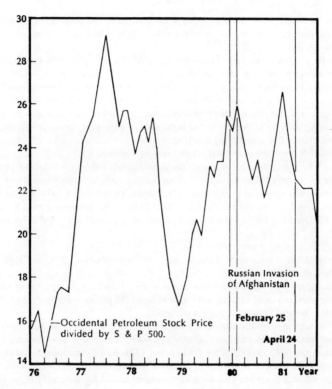

Source: Occidental Petroleum Co.

Figure 4.11 also indicates that, prior to the announcement of the lifting of the embargo, the stock market had increased while Occidental's price was declining. This uptick in the market can be explained by President Reagan's pro-free-trade position, and possibly because the news of the lifting of the embargo leaked to the press. The decline in the price of Occidental Petroleum stock may be explained by the securing of other sources of SPA by the Russians. The lifting of the embargo on wheat and SPA thus benefited the economy in general more than it benefited Occidental.

The available information suggests that the embargo had a minimal effect on the Soviet Union, while it imposed significant costs on Occidental.

NOTES

1. The basic agreement was to last three years. It called for the government of Japan to restrain its exports of complete color televisions to the U.S. to 1.56 million per year and of "incomplete" sets to 190,000 per year.

2. Under TSUSA (U.S. Tariff Structure) Item 807, if a U.S. firm ships color television parts abroad for assembly, only the value added is subject to a 5 percent tariff.

3. The argument here is that given the "comparative" advantage of foreign producers under free trade conditions, the penetration was inevitable. One could then argue that the strike weakened, at least temporarily, the protectionist pressures. Once the market was penetrated and protectionist policies were again in force, these would be in the form of preventing further penetration rather than undoing penetration that already had occurred.

4. *Annual Statistical Report 1968*, Department of Commerce.

5. The VRAs were intended to provide the domestic steel industry with several years in which to make the investments that would allow it to compete favorably with foreign producers. The agreement originally was scheduled to expire in 1971, but was extended until 1974. During this period, steel imports from Japan and the European Economic Community each were allowed to increase from the level of 5.75 million net tons at a rate of 5 percent per year until 1971, and 2.5 percent per year until 1974.

6. On this issue see Canto (1984).

7. For a technical discussion of this scenario, see Appendices A, B, C in Chapter 2.

8. Crandall, (1981) p. 29.

9. The trigger price was based on the Japanese steel industry's average cost of production or the five-year average rate of capacity utilization in Japan (85 percent). However, in 1977 the Japanese industry operated at only 72 percent of capacity.

10. The problem originally arose as a result of inherent contradictions in President Carter's policies. On one hand, he invited the steel industry to pursue relief through newly enacted amendments to the antidumping law contained in the Trade Act of 1974. At the same time, he asked the Council on Wage and Price Stability (COWPS) to prepare a report on the industry's condition. As a result of these actions, steel producers filed dumping complaints against Japanese and EEC producers. Furthermore, the COWPS report showed that Japanese firms did indeed enjoy a substantial cost advantage over U.S. producers. It also suggested that dumping complaints against European exporters probably would succeed. Thus, the Administration faced a major dilemma: If it processed the complaints, it could curtail exports of European steel to the U.S.; however, denying the Europeans access to the U.S. market would have endangered any chance of consummating the multilateral trade negotiation in progress at that time.

11. See the *Wall Street Journal*, "Steel Firms Will File Unfair-Trade Cases; Upheaval Seen in Markets for Some Time."

12. See "Commerce Finds Subsidies in Steel Investigations," *Commerce News*. "U.S. Plans for Duties on Some Steel Imports May Provide Little Help to Domestic Firms." *Wall Street Journal*.

13. "Commerce Unit Says Six Nations 'Dumping' Steel." *Wall Street Journal*.

14. "U.S. Rules European Steel Prices Unfair; Duties as High as 26 Percent May Be Imposed." *Wall Street Journal*.

15. "Commerce Unit Says Six Nations 'Dumping' Steel." *Wall Street Journal*.

16. "Europe Agrees to Cut Steel Exports to the U.S." *Wall Street Journal*.

17. *Annual Statistical Report*, American Iron and Steel Institute (Washington D.C., 1981).

18. For a thorough, theoretical discussion of the effects of quotas and tariffs see A.B. Laffer and M. Miles (1981).

19. "U.S. Tentatively Rules 3 Countries Subsidize Various Steel Exports." *Wall Street Journal*.

20. See V. A. Canto, (1984).

21. Imports of nonrubber footwear were restricted from Korea and Taiwan from July 1977 to June 1981. In a 1981 study, Joon Suh reported that under the restriction, the quantity of low-priced footwear fell more than the quantity of high-priced footwear, and that the prices of lower-priced shoes increased more than the prices of higher-priced shoes. He concludes: ''These findings are indicative of quantitative nature of the quotas.'' Because of the relative price increase of lower-priced products, Suh also concludes that the import restrictions were a regressive burden, affecting low-income consumers more adversely than wealthier buyers.

22. U.S. Department of Commerce, (December 1981).

23. Wharton Econometric Forecasting Associates (July 1983).

24. Bollman, Canto and Melich, (1982).

25. Canto, Eastin, Laffer and Turney, (1982).

26. Ibid.

27. See the Protocol between the Government of the U.S.S.R. and the Government of the Kingdom of Morocco on the Exchange of Some Commodities, *Foreign Trade* (February 1981).

28. ''U.S.S.R. Buys Superphosphoric Acid from Belgium.'' *Fertilizer International* (November 1981).

29. Source: Occidental Petroleum Corporation.

30. SPA and merchant acid are liquid fertilizers containing 70 percent and 54 percent of P_2O_5, respectively. DAP and TSP are granular fertilizers containing 46 percent P_2O_5. The only difference between DAP and TSP is nitrogen content. Tonnages that appear herein are expressed in terms of P_2O_5.

31. Source: Occidental Petroleum Corporation.

5

Empirical Determinants of Trade Restrictions

INTRODUCTION

In response to a combination of falling output and eroding market share, the steel industry has sought higher tariffs and other restrictions on steel imports from Europe and other foreign steel makers. As a result of the steel industry request in 1983, the International Trade Commission (ITC) recommended that import quotas and additional tarrifs be imposed on foreign steel in five major steel producing areas for the next five years.[1] However, this protection from foreign competition would be contingent upon the domestic steel industry's demonstrating a willingness to reduce costs, including wages, and to modernize its facilities.

Bethlehem Steel Corporation estimated that the steel quotas recommended by the ITC would produce a 10 percent price increase for steel sold in the U.S. and generate approximately $2 billion in cash flow to the domestic industry. Supposedly, the improved cash flow could be used to modernize existing facilities, this in turn making the industry competitive with foreign producers. Advocates argue that the restriction would be a giant step towards preserving jobs in the steel industry. On the face of it, political considerations seemed to dictate doing ''something'' to protect the steel industry. Thirty-six states produce steel and the nine largest producers—Indiana, Ohio, Pennsylvania, Michigan, Illinois, Kentucky, New York, California and Texas—have a total of 225 electoral votes.[2] Democratic presidential candidates actively campaigned for protecting the domestic steel industry. Similarly an argument can be made that the administration's pre-election decision to seek world-wide voluntary restraint was politically motivated.

Supporters of the president argue that he made the best out of a bad situation. They point to the fact that the steel companies were threatening to file dozens of lawsuits charging unfair practices and this, the president's supporters claim, would disrupt U.S. trade policy. Other evidence consistent with this view is that the industry was also pushing protectionist legislation in Congress. These efforts were reportedly dropped as a result of the administration's promise to restrict imports through bilateral negotiations.[3]

The steel industry experience points to the reduction in profits and employment in the steel industry as well as an increase in the market share of imported steel as the primary reasons for the increased lobbying for measures designed to protect the steel industry. The rationalization for this type of behavior is fairly straightforward. Trade restrictions give rise to economic rents, which in turn give rise to rent-seeking behavior. To the extent that different special interest groups who benefit from the protectionist actions can organize effectively, the political process may result in protectionist policies.[4]

Recently, Brock, Magee, and Young (1985) provided a theoretical justification that links the rise in protectionist policies in an industry to the industry employment and profits level as well as the market share of imports. The model focuses on a hierarchical game–theoretical approach that incorporates the role of three distinct special interest groups: workers, capital investors and political parties. Their model explores the behavior of lobbies and political parties in the setting of international commercial and industrial policy. In their framework, policies are set by political parties who are power brokers among special interest groups. Protectionist and anti-protectionist lobbies channel resources to their favored parties to maximize their probability of election.

Brock, Magee and Young's analysis suggest that special interest groups use political pressure to force the government to intervene when competition from abroad threatens the earnings of labor and capital in their industry. Thus within this framework it would not be surprising to find that developments of more general impact, such as a deterioration in the balance of trade, tend to provoke political interventions in trade policies. Whether changes in domestic profits, employment and/or increased imports penetration result in a rise in protectionism as implied by the previously discussed model is an empirically testable proposition.

The empirical analysis presented in this chapter focuses on two types of protectionist actions: industry-specific and across-the-broad trade actions. Policies aimed at protecting a particular industry are classified as microevents. Table 5.1 provides a summary listing of the microevents for the 1960–82 period. Similarly, across-the-board trade actions are classified as macroevents. Table 5.2 provides a listing of the macroevents for the 1960–82 period. Several of the macroevents listed in Table 5.2 deserve an explanation. The embargoes to the Soviet Union in 1980, and to the Soviet Union and Poland in 1981, in particular, were purely political events and may justifiably be excluded from the sample. For this reason we classified 1980 as a nonevent year. However, during 1978 and 1981, the U.S. negotiated major trade restrictions on the import of steel and automobiles. The impact of these restrictions on the economy easily justifies our classification of these dates as macroevents in our empirical analysis. In contrast, we classify 1975, the year in which Tokyo Round negotiations took place, as a nonevent year, because the most important negotiated results were never implemented.

EMPIRICAL METHODOLOGY

The major research technique employed by empirical studies in this area utilizes ordinary least square regression analysis performed on a cross-sectional basis. In contrast, our analysis of macroevents employs a time series analysis. The microevents are studies using a mixture of cross section and time series analysis.[5]

The dependent variable in both the macro- and microevent analysis was the qualitative variable indicating nonintervention or the imposition of trade restrictions. Given the qualitative nature of the dependent variable, logit analysis was chosen to predict a policy of trade intervention given measures of inquiry to industries affected by trade. The use of logit analysis is consistent with the use of this procedure in other applications.[6] Logit analysis estimates a logistic probability curve as a function of the explanatory variables. Since the dependent variables are binary and the function is nonlinear, maximum likelihood estimation techniques are used. Our estimates are based on the statistical analysis system logit routines. Logit makes only minimal requirements concerning the statistical properties of error terms in the regression. These requirements are met in the case of the political uncertainties associated with the intervention in trade which are the source of the stochastic error terms.

Microevents: Sample Selection

To implement the analysis on the microeconomic level, trade restrictions imposed since 1960 were classified according to the Standard In-

TABLE 5.1. Summary of the Microevents: 1960–82

1. Textiles (SIC*: 22)
   a. Established voluntary quotas limiting the importation of cotton textiles (1961).
   b. Voluntary quota on exports to the U.S. of woolen and synthetic fabric (1968).
   c. Multifiber Arrangement restricted textile imports (1974).
2. Sheet Glass and Carpets (SIC: 227)
   Raised tariffs on sheet glass and carpets (1962).
3. Meat (SIC: 201)
   a. Meat Import Act of 1964 designed to protect domestic cattle industry; quotas come into effect when imports exceed adjusted base by 10 percent (trigger level); president may elect to suspend quotas.
   b. Informal restraints on major meat-supplying countries; special bilateral restrictions with Honduras (1969).
   c. Voluntary restraints on meat imports negotiated with additional countries (1970).
   d. Restraint program on meat continued, allowing for 1971 imports to be higher than the suspended trigger level but below negotiated restraint levels (1971).
   e. Voluntary restraints negotiated on meat (1972).
   f. Voluntary restraint negotiated on meat (1975).
   g. Voluntary restrictions on meat imports negotiated (1977).
4. Financial Institutions (SIC: 60)
   a. The Interest Equalization Tax, designed to restrict the availability to foreigners of banking services in the United States (mid-1960s).
   b. Foreign Direct Investment Program, designed to restrict U.S. financing of foreign direct investments by U.S. firms (mid-1960s).
5. Steel (SIC: 331)
   a. Voluntary Restraint Agreement imposed on imports of steel (1969).
   b. Voluntary Restraint Agreement on steel extended from 1971 to 1974 (1972).
   c. Trigger Price Mechanism on steel implemented (1978).
   d. Steel quotas negotiated with European countries (1982).
6. Specialty Steel (SIC: 332)
   a. Tariffs on stainless steel flatware raised (1971).
   b. Quotas placed on specialty steel (1976).
7. Fruit (SIC: 017)
   a. Negotiated voluntary quotas on Mexican fruit and vegetables (1971) allowed to lapse (1982).
8. Soybean (SIC: 0116)
   a. U.S. soybean export embargo (1974).
9. Nonrubber Footwear (SIC: 314)
   a. Orderly Marketing Agreement negotiated with Korea and Taiwan to restrict imports of nonrubber footwear to 1976 levels.
10. Color TVs (SIC: 365)
    a. Orderly Marketing Agreement with Japan to restrict imports of color televisions (1977).
    b. Orderly Marketing Agreement with Korea and Taiwan to restrict imports of color televisions (1980).
11. Industrial Fasteners (SIC: 3452)
    a. Restraints on imports of industrial fasteners, after once failing at the ITC, were imposed; the commission was required to consider it again following Ways and

TABLE 5.1. *(continued)*

Means Committee request (1979).

12. Lightweight Chassis Trucks (SIC: 3713)

a. 25 percent tariff imposed on lightweight chassis trucks (1980).

13. Automobiles (SIC: 3711)

a. "Voluntary" export restraints negotiated with Japan to restrict automobile imports (1980).

14. Motorcycles (SIC: 375)

a. Harley-Davidson seeks U.S. trade protection from Japanese imports (1982).

*SIC is the abbreviated form of Standard Industrial Code.

TABLE 5.2. Summary of the Macroevents: 1960–82

1. Trade Expansion Act of 1962 which gave president the authority to reduce tariffs of July 1, 1962 by 50 percent in 5 years (1) allowed elimination of U.S. and European Economic Community, together accounting for 80 percent of free world exports; (2) selected agricultural commodities where changes would assure some increase in U.S. exports of like goods; (3) tropical agricultural forestry products not produced in the U.S. if the European Economic Community would reciprocate; (4) articles which had an ad valorem rate of 5 percent.

2. The sixth GATT tarriff conference, 1962, known as the Kennedy Round; authorized 50 percent tariff reductions on most industrial products and 30 percent to 50 percent on others.

3. President Nixon, in August 1971, ordered the gold window closed and imposed an across-the-board 10 percent increase in tariffs.

4. Trade Act of 1974 provided safeguards for American industry and American workers from unfair or injurious important competition; provided "adjustment assistance" for industries or workers hurt by imports.

5. Tokyo Round, in 1975, attempted to constrain nontariff barriers; negotiations designed to liberalize international trade. Since the most important negotiations were never implemented, the Tokyo Round will not be included in the list of events used in the empirical analysis.

6. Canadian imports negotiated for first time in 1977.

7. Trade Act of 1979 overhauled U.S. countervailing duty laws designed to protect domestic industries against foreign government subsidies on imported goods; domestic industries required to show injury by subsidized imports before offsetting duty would be imposed; speeding investigations and imposition of penalties under countervailing duty and anti-dumping laws; established new customs valuation which used price actually paid for merchandise when sold for exportation to U.S.; discouraged discrimination against foreign suppliers bidding for government purchase; curbing use of standards as disguised trade barriers.

8. Shipments to the Soviet Union, in 1980, of wheat, superphosphoric acid and other products embargoed.

9. Embargoes in 1981 on exports requiring validated licenses for shipment to Poland and the Soviet Union.

dustrial Classification (SIC) industry most affected by the trade restriction (as shown in Table 5.1). The trade restriction was categorized as a tariff (price restriction) or a quota (quantity restriction). However in the empirical analysis, only the absence or presence of a restriction was recognized (i.e., 0, 1 binary classification).

For each industry affected by trade policy, ten years of historical data on employment, imports, and return on capital were obtained. The sources for the employment and import measures were SIC classifications of employment in industries and imports. The Center of the Study of Security Prices (CRSP) file of returns by SIC code provided the industry average stock returns. After netting out industries for which inadequate data were available, 14 industries were included in the sample (Table 5.1). In addition to the sample of industries directly affected by trade policy, a matching sample of industries not affected by trade policy was selected at random.

The data for statistical analysis of microeffects were constructed from the sample of industries affected by trade policy as follows. First, growth rate of employment and changes in growth rates were computed for the two years prior to the intervention of trade policy. Growth rates were then expressed as the difference between the SIC industry employment growth and the U.S. aggregate growth in employment, and growth in SIC imports relative to total U.S. import growth. One observation consists therefore of the qualitative designation of trade intervention (typically, quota), the growth rate in employment, and the relative change in the growth of imports expressed as differences from the national averages and the associated SIC industry stock returns net of the aggregate market returns.

Macroevents: Sample Selection

To examine generalized macroeconomic trade interventions, annual data on changes in the real balance of trade, employment and the real rate of return on common stocks were collected. The policy actions are those given in Table 5.2. A policy action having a generalized trade-reducing effect in a given year is the event to be explained and the dependent variable takes the value of unity; otherwise it is zero. The period of analysis is 1960–82 (23 observations).

THE DETERMINANTS OF INDUSTRY-SPECIFIC TRADE POLICIES: THE MICROEVENTS

The results reported in Table 5.3 suggest that the industry employment performance relative to the national economy has a positive and significant effect on the successful implementation of industry-specific trade restrictions. Notice also that although somewhat weaker, the stock return variable yields results similar to those of the employment variable. These two results are quite interesting for they suggest a nonadversarial relationship between workers and capital owners when it comes to lobbying for protectionist policies for their industries. Finally, the results also suggest that import penetration does not appear to have a significant impact on industry-specific trade policies.

Decline in employment in particular industries relative to the aggregate U.S. experience significantly increases the probablity of a trade-reducing policy intervention. This outcome, no doubt, reflects the fact that specific industry effects can be used to mobilize pressure from well-defined interest groups. Comparability of the empirical results reported in this chapter with the results reported in the literature is somewhat of a problem. The reason is that the bulk of the literature uses ordinary least square cross-sectional analysis to estimate the effects of pressure groups on trade. Fortunately in a recent paper Ray (1981) reports ordinary least square and profit cross-sectional analysis of the U.S. trade restriction for the year 1970. Although Ray's analysis uses a larger number of explanatory variables than ours (such as capital intensity, concentration ratio, and fraction of labor force that is skilled), it does not include a measure of total labor employment nor of profitability. This is really unfortunate since our results for the microevents identify employment and profits as significant explanatory variables in the determination of industry-specific trade restrictions. However, Ray's results indicate that for specific industries (i.e., microevents), the percent change in imports does not play a significant role. The result is similar to that obtained in our analysis.

TABLE 5.3. Results of Logit Estimation: The Microevents.
Trade-Reducing Policy Intervention (dependent variable = 1).

Independent Variable	Coefficient	Standard Error	Significance
Intercept	−1.269	.355	0.0004
Relative growth rate in employment*	−9.616	5.36	0.073
Relative stock returns*	−2.97	1.42	0.074
Relative growth rate in imports*	1.83	1.67	0.197
Model Chi-Square	4.58		0.1260

*All variables calculated relative to the national average.

EMPIRICAL DETERMINANTS OF ACROSS-THE-BOARD TRADE RESTRICTIONS: THE MACROEVENTS

The estimated logit function reported in Table 5.4 suggests that whenever the trade balance deteriorates the probability of a trade-reducing initiative is increased. This result we attribute to the pervasiveness of mercantilist policies deeply ingrained in the popular press which link trade balace deficit with a "net export" of jobs. However, it is quite interesting to note that broader effects of trade, such as reduced employment growth and/or a decline in the stock market are not associated with generalized trade-reducing policy actions. Thus the results suggest that generalized interventions in trade policy are most likely to occur when there is a deteriorating trade balance.

CONCLUSIONS

Trade policies appear to be systematically related to economic events. The empirical results reported in this chapter show that specific industry trade policies are directly related to those interest groups directly affected by competition from abroad. Relative slow growth or a decline in employment and/or profitability in an industry tend to increase the probability of a policy that will reduce international trade in that industry. The nature of the restriction may in part depend on the ability to circumvent the GATT Agreements. To the extent that the U.S. desires to maintain some semblance of abiding by GATT, orderly marketing agreements or quotas will be imposed to protect domestic employment.

The movement from a commitment to free trade following World War II to so-called "fair" trade in the 1970s is a reflection of the political cloud of pressure groups. The movement towards "fair" trade has meant an increasing use of specific trade restrictions. The legislative atmosphere for such intrusions into the free flow of goods has been facilitated by the Trade Act of 1974, which no longer requires that industries show that imports were the major cause of injury.

Given the significance of relative employment growth rates and the inevitability of dynamic changes in employment in various sectors of the economy, a certain pessimism concerning the future of free trade and the efficient allocation of resources across national boundaries is warranted. On the other hand, even though at the microlevel the concern is with the aggregate employment and profit levels (i.e., the competitiveness of the

TABLE 5.4. Results of Logit Estimation: The Macroevents.
Trade-Reducing Policy Intervention (dependent variable = 1).

Independent Variable	Coefficient	Standard Error	Significance
Intercept	−3.14	2.13	.139
Trade balance as a share of GNP	−4.22	1.89	.026
Real stock returns	−9.9	6.4	.124
Percent change in employment	−.057	0.779	.940
Model chi-square	17.54		.0005

U.S. economy) the logit estimation suggests generalized or macroeconomic trade policy interventions are not most immediately affected by a slowing in employment growth and/or decline in the stock market. Rather, the most important determinant of major trade-reducing policies since 1960 has been a deteriorating trade balance.

NOTES

1. See Lachica and Boyle (1984).
2. See Farnsworth (1984a, b).
3. See Pine (1984b).
4. For a discussion on the politics of special interest groups, see Brock and Magee (1978). The analysis of the rent-seeking behavior can be traced to Krueger's (1974) seminal paper. Krueger's analysis has been further refined and generalized by Bhagwati and Srinivasan (1980).
5. An excellent summary of the theoretical and empirical literature can be found in Lavergne (1983).
6. See Amemiya (1981) for a review of the use of qualitative choice models.

6
The Stock Market, Employment, and Protectionism

INTRODUCTION

If an industrial trade policy is to be of any value, as far as protection of jobs and preserving equity value is concerned, then the implementation of trade policies is likely to cause growth and increased profitability in the protected industry. The industry stock market index, a proxy for equity value, will experience a rise (i.e., the return on the index will also rise). On the other hand, if the trade actions impact the whole economy (i.e., across-the-board trade restrictions), the impact of the trade policies will be reflected in the equity values of the stock market (i.e., S&P 500 index).

Following a period of rapid economic growth known as the "roaring '20s," Congress, in 1929 and 1930, passed the largest tax on traded products in the history of the United States. The stock market "crash of '29" and the worldwide phenomenon of the Great Depression followed immediately. The grim experience of the Smoot-Hawley tariffs in the 1930s is interpreted by some as ample demonstration that protectionism carries with it major implications for the economy.[1]

Whether protectionist policies improve the performance of an industry and/or the economy is an empirical issue. The objective of this paper is to determine empirically the effects of protectionist policies. The results will allow us to discriminate between the competing hypotheses.

STOCK MARKET AND PROTECTIONISM: A CASUAL LOOK

A casual examination of the performance of the stock market and the announcements of trade restrictions lends support to the view that protectionist policies reduce equity values.

Early declines in the Dow Jones Industrial Average (DJI) of between 16 and 20 points coincided with 1982 announcements of the administration's "get tough" policies in trade and a new initiative by the steel industry to seek protection against foreign competitors[2] (Table 6.1). Similarly, during 1983, on the day new restrictions on specialty steel were announced, the DJI fell 16.7 points. A week later, when the U.S. International Trade Commission (ITC) had ruled that imports of frozen orange juice concentrate from Brazil were injuring U.S. producers, the Dow industrials fell 17.02 points.

A similar litany applies to the rout in equity values during 1984. The stage was set when a Wall Street Journal story on January 6 reported how election year concerns and and last minute arguments by Commerce Secretary Malcolm Baldridge persuaded the president to overrule a cabinet group and support a strict import relief program for the domestic industry. Although the market actually rose that day, hitting its peak of 1286.64, it was downhill from then on.

On January 10, the day of the first big decline in the market, the European Economic Community reported it was close to announcing specific retaliatory measures in response to U.S. imposition of restrictions

TABLE 6.1. Trade Policy and the Stock Market

Date	Headline	Change in Dow Jones Industrials
Jan. 5	"Reaganites Plan Trade Offensive to Prod Europe, Japan to Admit More U.S. Goods." *Wall Street Journal* (January 5, 1982).	− 17.22
Jan. 11	"Steel Firms Will File Unfair Trade Cases; Upheaval Seen in Markets for Some Items." *Wall Street Journal* (January 11, 1982).	− 16.07
Feb. 1	"Brock Calls for Fair Foreign Trade; Moves Close to Endorsing 'Reciprocity' Between Nations." *Los Angeles Times* (February 2, 1982).	− 19.41
Feb. 8	"U.S. Weighs Trade Actions Against Japan." *Wall Street Journal* (February 9, 1982).	− 17.60

on specialty steel.[3] Between January 12 and January 31, when the market declined 59 points, news of a raft of protectionist measures reached the market including:

- France's Finance Minister, Jacques Delors, said that European countries should consider imposing penalties on capital outflows to the U.S. if the dollar continued to rise on foreign exchange markets.[4]
- The European Economic Community disclosed new restrictions to be imposed upon U.S. imports in retaliation for U.S. restrictions on specialty steel. The administration described the EEC action as "economically unwise" but "politically necessary" for the Europeans—in effect, accepting this deterioration in free trade as the new status quo.[5]
- The U.S. ITC was investigating the impact of Canadian imports on the U.S. fish business. The Canadian government effectively nationalized its East Coast fisheries December 1983. The inquiry could lead to countervailing duties.[6]
- The U.S. proposed tighter standards on export licenses of high-tech products in an effort to stop militarily useful technology from being diverted to the Soviet Union. The immediate result was to anger European industrialists and government officials who viewed the new standards as hurtful to European competitiveness.[7]
- The Japanese government was reported to be considering new restrictions on imports of computer software and sophisticated telecommunications services.[8]
- Quotas on shoe imports were requested in a joint petition filed by management and labor of the U.S. shoe industry.[9]
- Bethlehem Steel Corporation and the United Steel Workers of America filed a petition with the U.S. ITC to reduce carbon steel imports from all countries to 15 percent of the U.S. market from their current 22 percent.[10]
- Democratic presidential candidate Walter Mondale articulated a policy of protectionist initiatives, including reciprocity, subsidizing exports and endorsement of a law restricting car sales to only those units with a high percentage of "local content" or value added from domestic labor and capital.[11]
- U.S.–Canadian talks broke down on a treaty for salmon fishing.[12]

The February 1–9 period also was marked by a plethora of initiatives aimed at restricting trade and news that aided those who backed protectionist measures.

- The Japanese trade surplus in 1983 grew to a record $31.65 billion from $18.08 billion in 1982.
- The Pentagon sought new powers to restrict exports of sensitive U.S. technology, such as computer and machine tools, to friendly and neutral countries.[13]
- The Commerce Department announced its preliminary ruling that Argentina, Brazil and Mexico have illegally subsidized their steel exports to the U.S. As a result, countervailing duties of 6.03 percent on Argentinian imports, 27.42 percent on Brazilian imports and 4.98 percent on Mexican imports are threatened.[14]
- Chairman of the Council of Economic Advisors Martin Feldstein opened up a new assault on free trade by asserting in the Economic Report of the President that the trade imbalance represented yet another ''structural deficit.'' Because of the budget deficit, the argument goes, the dollar is stronger than it otherwise would be. As capital flows into the U.S., the trade deficit widens. As a result, the burden of crowding out induced by the Federal deficit is borne disproportionately by import-competing and export industries.

February 8, the day the DJI fell 24 points, was an especially bad day on the trade front. That day, David Roderick, Chairman of the U.S. Steel Corporation, said the steel industry planned to file a ''tremendous'' number of complaints over unfair trade practices. The filings are part of an overall strategy, first signaled by Bethlehem Steel's request for overall quotas to secure quotas on foreign steel imports from all countries. In the opening round of this new assault, Roderick announced preparations were under way to file suit or otherwise seek trade actions against Argentina, Australia, Finland, Spain, South Africa, South Korea, Sweden, Romania and Venezuela.[15]

Moreover, momentum toward creating an anti-free-trade environment in Washington was given a boost by Fed Chairman Paul Volcker in both the Federal Reserve Board's Monetary Policy Report to Congress released February 6, and in his testimony to the House Banking Committee on February 8. In both instances, Volcker embraced Feldstein's linking the federal budget deficit to the strong dollar and the trade imbalance. In addition, Volcker provided a new image—one of the U.S. becoming a debtor nation—to those who argue for tax increases and trade protection. Said Volcker:

> It is ominous that the recorded net investment position of the United States overseas, built up gradually over the entire post-war period, will in the space of

only three years—1983, 1984, and 1985—be reserved. If the data at all reflect reality, the largest and richest economy in the world is on the verge of becoming a net debtor internationally and would soon become the largest.[16]

A FRAMEWORK TO MEASURE THE IMPACT OF TRADE POLICY

In an efficient market, the equity value of an industry reflects the future output and potential future profits. If an expansion is anticipated, at the initial stages of the expansion the industries will consume more than they produce. That is, capital equipment will be purchased and installed. Following this logic, for the country as a whole the anticipated expansion will, under a floating exchange rate, result in a deterioration of the trade balance and a capital inflow. If the capital market anticipates the future expansion and growth in the industry (economy), the equity values may in the short run exceed the replacement cost of capital. This suggests that changes in the equity values of an industry or for the stock market as a whole, to a large extent, are reflections in the changes in expectations about the future growth prospects of the industry and the economy.

From the vantage point of the protected industries, if a trade restriction or industrial policy is to be of any value, the policy must preserve the jobs and/or the profitability of the industries affected by the industrial policy. In this case, one will expect the stock return and/or employment performance to experience an increase around the time when the protectionist policies are announced. Thus observation of the stock and employment performance around the announcement and implementation of the industrial policy, should help us to understand the impact of the trade action. This concept has been used extensively in the finance and accounting literature to analyze the impact of "events" on stock returns.

The Mean Value Model Test

The "event time methodology" pioneered by Fama, Fisher, Jensen and Roll (1969) requires an equilibrium model of the expected change in equity value (i.e., the rate of return).

Merton (1980) and LeRoy (1982) have suggested alternative models to estimate the expected rate of return of aggregated equity indices. One commonly used model, which will be adopted in this study, is the mean value model.

The expected return on an index is estimated by taking the mean value of the returns over a specified time length prior to the event period. Then the mean value is applied outside the event period. Any deviation from the expected return is attributed to the trade action. Therefore, these forecast errors (i.e., deviations from the mean) are used as a proxy for the event-related abnormal performance.

The length of the event period is usually chosen arbitrarily. For purposes of this study the event period spans 12 months preceding the announcement of the trade action and the 6 months following the announcement of the trade action. For a particular industry event with more than one trade action, event periods are aligned by pivoting the data around the announcement time. The average prediction error (APE) is calculated as follows:

$$(1) \qquad APE_t = \frac{1}{J_t} \sum_{j=t}^{J=k} PE_{jt}$$

where J_t is the number of trade actions selected, t denotes time relative to the event period, PE_{jt} denotes the prediction error for the particular event in the t month.

The statistical significance of the abnormal performance is determined by constructing a statistic for the cumulative average prediction error (CAPE), where

$$(2) \qquad CAPE_{t1,t2} = \sum_{t=t_1}^{t_2} APE_t$$

Significance of the CAPE is determined by the "t-test" statistics, calculated from the ratio of the cumulative average preduction error to its estimated standard deviation.[17] The standard deviation is estimated from the time series of the industry index. The major problem with the estimation of the t-statistic is the time series dependency of the data used to estimate the variance. Most event studies have ignored this issue. However, if the prediction errors exhibit first order autocorrelation, the variance of CAPE will be undervalued. In cases where there is first order autocorrelation, the following formula will be used to estimate the variance.[18]

$$(3) \qquad Var\ (CAPE_{t1,t2}) = t\ Var\ (APE_t) + 2\ \frac{t-1}{t}\ Cov(APE_t,\ APE_{t+1})$$

A second major problem arising from the estimation of the variance in event studies, is the evidence that the variance of the stock return increases around the event announcement.[19] This will result in an underestimation of the true t-test values.[20] We shall use the event period, a high variance period, to estimate the variance of the CAPE. This will cause our results to be on the conservative side and this, as we shall see later, will not affect the thrust of our results.

Another problem may arise if an incorrect universal event period is imposed for all the events selected. It has been argued that arbitrary choice of event period may lead to suboptimal results (see Brown, Lockwood and Summer (1983)). Despite the possibility of bias in parameter estimation due to misspecified event period, most event time studies have used an arbitrary universal event period for estimating event-related effect. In order to minimize the problem, one should ideally estimate maximum likelihood of event period for each of the policies or events selected. One possible reason for expecting changing event period is that speed of information dissemination and efficiency of adaptation to events for an industry or a firm may be changing over time. We believe these changes are likely to be more pronounced for a firm than for an industry as a whole, or the economy in aggregate. In our study, though we are imposing universal event period, the impact of possible misspecification is being minimized by examining the event effect over three different intervals in the event period. In addition, we are using only aggregated industrial indices which are more likely to be consistently efficient.

THE EFFECT OF TRADE POLICIES ON INDUSTRIAL STOCK INDICES

For the purpose of this study we have selected, in addition to the aggregate economy, four industries: (1) leather shoes, (2) steel, (3) color TVs and, (4) automobiles. In Table 6.2 we provide a brief summary of statistics for the 1960–82 period, for the stock market index (S&P 500) and four respective industrial stock indicies aggregated over a 3-digit code.[21]

The Macroevents and the Stock Market

Table 6.3 provides a brief summary of the macroevents considered. For the empirical examination of the impact of macroevents or trade actions, we analyze changes in the S&P 500 index surrounding the event announcement month as reported in the *Wall Street Journal*.

TABLE 6.2. Expected Return Estimates from Mean Market Model, 1960–82

Index	Entire Period	Bear Periods	Bull Periods
S&P 500	0.0075	− 0.0219	0.0172
	(0.0428)	(0.0415)	(0.389)
Shoes	0.0145	− 0.0226	0.0259
	(0.0639)	(0.0596)	(0.0609)
Steel	0.0074	− 0.0190	0.0155
	(0.0634)	(0.0590)	(0.0628)
TV	0.0109	− 0.0212	0.0209
	(0.0596)	(0.0526)	(0.0583)
Auto	0.0101	0.0215	0.0199
	(0.0563)	(0.0526)	(0.0539)

In Table 6.4 we present the cumulative average prediction errors (CAPE) resulting from applying the mean value model for three different intervals in the event period. The first interval starts 12 months preceding the event and ends six months following the event (EM − 12 to EM + 6). The second interval examined includes 12 months up to and inclusive of the event month (EM − 12 to EM − 0). The third interval includes 12 months prior to the event month (EM − 12 to EM − 1). Upon inspection of Table 6.4, it is apparent that the CAPE has been consistently negative in the second (EM − 12 to EM − 0) and third (EM − 12 to

TABLE 6.3. Summary of Macroevents

Event Date	Market Type	Brief Description
08/71	bull	Gold Window closed and an across-the-board ten percent increase in tariffs
12/74	bull	Trade act of 1974 (adjustment assistance for industries or workers hurt by imports)
03/77	bull	Canadian imports negotiated
07/78	bull	Implemented trigger price mechanism on steel imports
11/79	bull	Trade Act of 1979 (countervailing duty laws to protect domestic industries against subsidized imports)
11/81	bull	Embargo on exports to Poland and Soviet Union

TABLE 6.4. Cumulative Average Prediction Error for Macroevent-Related Time Periods for Trade Policies

CAPE Period	Entire Period		Bull Periods	
	CAPE	t	CAPE	t
EM − 12 to EM + 6	0.0185	.23	− 0.1886	1.11
EM − 12 to EM − 0	− .0668	1.01	− 0.1857	2.34
EM − 12 to EM − 1	− .0815	1.2	− 0.1822	2.32
Average (APE)*	0.0011		− .0057	
Var. (APE)*	0.00033		.0005	

*The statistics reported in the table were calculated using the EM − 12 to EM + 6 interval.

EM − 1) intervals, across all the panels. The result is consistent with two alternative hypotheses:

1. The decline in stock returns gives rise to protectionist pressures.
2. The stock returns decline in anticipation of the trade restriction.

In chapter 5 we analyzed the empirical determinants of trade restrictions, where the empirical analysis failed to uncover any evidence in favor of the hypothesis that a declining stock market results in protectionist measures. In fact, most of the selected trade restrictions were announced in bull market periods.[22] Taken at face value, the results leave us with the possibility that the decline in the stock index occurs in anticipation of the forthcoming trade restriction. The low t-values for the CAPE, calculated by applying mean value model over the entire period, suggest that the effects of trade policies are not statistically significant. However, since most of the macroevents occurred during the bull market periods and by definition, stock returns are expected to rise during the bull market periods, we reexamined the results by considering bull period effect. The estimate of the expected return is obtained by applying the mean value model over the bull market period alone. The evidence suggests a negative and significant decline in the stock returns in anticipation of the trade restriction. For the whole sample, though the t-statistic is at best marginally improved given the variance increase around the event time, the t-statistics tend to be biased downwards. The evidence may be interpreted as suggesting that across-the-board restrictive trade actions may have had a small but adverse effect on the stock market. There is no evidence suggesting the desired positive effect on the equity predicted by the advocates of protectionist policies.

The Microevents and the Industry Stock Index

In this section we analyze the effect of microevents on the selected industries. The sample selection was based on the availability of the data during the period in question. The list of the events selected is shown in Table 6.5.[23] The empirical analysis of the impact of the microevents on industries is conducted in a fashion similar to the analysis of macroevents. The CAPE is calculated for the specific industry for three intervals in the event period.

In Table 6.6 CAPE for the leather footwear industry is presented. The CAPE is consistently negative. Notice that when the expected values for the event period are estimated by applying the mean value model over the entire period, CAPE are fairly small with insignificant t values. Given that most of the microevents took place during the bull market periods, we reestimated the event period expected return by applying the mean value model over bull market periods. The results are shown in the second column; notice that the t-statistics improved substantially.

TABLE 6.5. Summary of Microevents

Event Date	Market Type	
1. Steel Industry (SIC 331)		
01/69	bear	Voluntary restraints on import of steel.
01/71	bull	Voluntary restraints imposed were extended.
01/76	bull	Quotas on specialty steel imposed.
01/77	bull	Quotas on specialty steel continued.
04/78	bull	Trigger price mechanism implemented.
10/78	bull	Trigger price mechanism is further tightened.
10/82	bear	Quotas on imports of steel from Europe.
2. Color TV (SIC 365)		
03/77	bull	Restriction on import of TVs from Japan.
01/79	bull	Reduction in export of TVs from Taiwan.
06/80	bull	Restriction on export of TVs from Japan and Taiwan.
3. Automobiles (SIC 3711)		
08/80	bull	25% tariff increase on light trucks.
06/79	bull	Auto imports from Japan curbed.
4. Nonrubber Footwear (SIC 314)		
06/77	bull	Restriction on imports of shoes.

TABLE 6.6. Cumulative Average Prediction Error for Microevent-Related Time Periods: The Footwear Industry

CAPE Period	Entire Period		Bull Periods	
	CAPE	t	CAPE	t
EM − 12 to EM + 6	− .0239	0.12	− .2533	1.90
EM − 12 to EM − 0	− .11876	.75	− .2679	1.69
EM − 12 to EM − 1	− .0180	1.19	− .3174	2.1
Average APE*	− .0012		− .0127	
Autocorr.			− .215	
Var. (APE)*			.0019	

*The statistics reported in the table were calculated using the EM − 12 to EM + 6 interval.

The significant t-statistics lead us to accept the hypothesis that the imposition of the protectionist trade policies in the leather shoe industry have had a detrimental effect on the shoe industry equity value.

Next, the effects of trade restrictions on the industrial stock indicies of color TV, automobile and steel industries are examined. The CAPE and the related statistics are reported in Tables 6.7, 6.8 and 6.9. The results are qualitatively similar to the ones obtained for the leather shoe industry, i.e., the restrictive trade policies have been detrimental to the equity values of these industries as well.

TABLE 6.7. Cumulative Average Prediction Error for Microevent-Related Time Periods: The Color TV Industry

CAPE Period	Entire Period		Bull Periods	
	CAPE	t	CAPE	t
EM − 12 to EM + 6	− .0419	.30	− .2305	1.6
EM − 12 to EM − 0	− .0949	.86	− .2340	2.1
EM − 12 to EM − 1	− .1049	.95	− .2420	2.2
Average APE*	− .0022		− .01213	
Autocorr.	.153		− .153	
Var. (APE)*	.001		.0010	

*The statistics reported in the table were calculated using the EM − 12 to EM + 6 interval.

TABLE 6.8. Cumulative Average Prediction Error for Microevent-Related Time Periods: The Auto Industry Industry

CAPE Period	Entire Period		Bull Periods	
	CAPE	t	CAPE	t
EM − 12 to EM + 6	− .0419	.30	− .2571	1.6
EM − 12 to EM − 0	− .0949	.86	− .01684	1.2
EM − 12 to EM − 1	− .1049	.95	− .1723	1.3
Average APE*	− .0036		− .0128	
Autocorr.	− .215		.043	
Var. (APE)*	− .0019		.0014	

*The statistics reported in the table were calculated using the EM − 12 to EM + 6 interval.

THE EFFECT OF TRADE POLICIES ON EMPLOYMENT

The impact of trade policies on the equity values, as examined via changes in stock indicies, describes the effect of the trade actions on the owners' capital. However, capital is only one of the inputs of the production process. Another input variable of particular interest is labor. In this section we examine the impact of trade policies on the labor employment in aggregate and in specific industries.

In Table 6.10 we present the mean growth in employment during different periods for selected industries and the economy as a whole. Total employment is measured as the total number of hours worked in a month.

TABLE 6.9. Cumulative Average Prediction Error for Microevent-Related Time Periods: The Steel Industry

CAPE Period	Entire Period		Bull Periods	
	CAPE	t	CAPE	t
EM − 12 to EM + 6	− .046	.38	− .1174	.98
EM − 12 to EM − 0	− .0298	.29	− .1361	1.36
EM − 12 to EM − 1	− .0116	.12	− .1096	1.10
Average APE*	− .0023		− .0587	
Autocorr.	.213		.213	
Var. (APE)*	.007		.0007	

*The statistics reported in the table were calculated using the EM − 12 to EM + 6 interval.

TABLE 6.10. Employment Growth

| Industry | SIC | Mean Growth in Employment | | | |
		Overall Period	Bull Period	Bear Period	Time Period
Steel	331	− 0.297	− 0.434	0.052	1/68
		(3.88)	(4.25)	(2.74)	12/81
Auto	3711	− 0.532	− 0.353	− 0.988	1/63
		(8.93)	(9.75)	(6.43)	
Shoe	314	− 0.368	− 0.186	− 1.52	12/81
		(4.17)	(4.12)	(4.52)	
TV	365	− 0.218	− 0.176	− 0.371	12/78
		(4.42)	(4.64)	(5.93)	
Nonagricultural		.1436	.15448	.11614	1980/1982
Employment		(1.023)	(.0869)	(1.352)	

For an empirical examination of the impact of the trade actions on employment, we have used the mean value model for the growth in the employment over the entire period and during the bull market periods, to estimate the expected value of growth in employment in the event period. Essentially, we are following an approach parallel to one used to examine the effect of trade policies on the equity values.

Macroevents and Employment

The empirical examination of the impact of macroevents on the gross nonagriculture employment in the economy is reported in Table 6.11. The

TABLE 6.11. Cumulative Average Prediction Error among U.S. Nonagricultural Employment Growth

| CAPE Period | Entire Period | | Bull Periods | |
	CAPE	t	CAPE	t
EM − 12 to EM + 6	− .2999	− 0.10	− .4312	− .19
EM − 12 to EM − 0	− 1.6887	− 0.72	− 1.7740	− .75
EM − 12 to EM − 1	− 0.3050	− 0.10	− .4345	− .13
Average (APE)*	− .0779		− .0887	
Autocorr.	− .46		− .46	
(APE)*	− .2615		− .2615	

*The statistics reported in the table were calculated using the EM − 12 to EM + 6 interval.

CAPE in employment growth is consistently negative for all three intervals considered. This is consistent with contentions that trade restrictions reduce the economy's efficiency and employment level. However, it must be noted that none of the CAPE is statistically significant and results do not change when CAPE is reestimated with the expected value estimated by applying the mean value model over the bull periods. Therefore, evidence is not sufficiently strong to reject the two alternative hypotheses regarding the effect of protectionist trade policy on employment growth and level.

Microevents and the Industrial Employment

The average cumulative prediction errors for the selected four industries are presented in Tables 6.12 and 6.13. The CAPE for all three intervals in the event period is consistently negative except for the steel industry. However, the negative values of CAPE are not statistically significant. The nature of results remains essentially similar when the employment growth is estimated over the bull market periods. Notice that irrespective of the sample chosen, for the steel industry the CAPE is significantly positive. Although these results suggest that restrictive micro trade policies have not resulted in gain in employment in the automobile, TV and shoe industries, they clearly suggest that trade restrictions may have resulted in higher employment in the steel industry.

SUMMARY

The results obtained from this study are quite interesting. We found decline in equity value and labor employment around the policy or macroevent's announcement time. Though the measured declines were not statistically significant, the tendency for equity value changes and employment growth to be positive—a minimum requirement for any effective trade policy—was certainly not evident.

The result for the microevents indicate a deterioration of equity values in the leather shoe, color TV, and automobile industries. The employment performance, around the policies' announcements, have appeared to be negatively affected. However, in most cases the results were not statistically significant, the exception being the steel industry, where positive growth in employment did materialize.

In conclusion, the evidence from the microevents study shows that

TABLE 6.12. Cumulative Average Prediction Error in Employment for Microevents— Entire Period Model for Employment Growth

CAPE Period	Steel		Automobile		TV		Shoe	
	CAPE	t	CAPE	t	CAPE	t	CAPE	t
EM−12 to EM−0	12.33	1.62	−21.00	−1.05	−10.53	.71	−8.71	−0.58
EM−12 to EM+6	8.93	0.97	−23.71	−0.95	−9.09	.52	−11.11	−0.63
EM−12 to EM−1	13.30	1.82	−21.65	−1.12	−10.05	.70	−8.37	−.59
Average (APE)	0.47		−1.24		−0.472		−.585	
Var. (APE)	4.39		30.18		14.86		15.99	
Autocorr.	−0.072		−.1402		−.310		−.21	

TABLE 6.13. Cumulative Average Prediction Errors In Employment for Microevents— Bull Period Model for Employment Growth

CAPE Period	Steel		Automobile		TV		Shoe	
	CAPE	t	CAPE	t	CAPE	t	CAPE	t
EM−12 to EM−0	10.55	1.41	−18.57	−0.92	−8.17	−0.55	−6.490	.44
EM−12 to EM+6	6.33	0.68	−20.31	−0.84	−5.64	−0.322	−10.315	−.585
EM−12 to EM−1	11.66	1.60	−19.50	−1.01	−7.87	−0.552	−8.186	−.558
Average (APE)	0.333		−1.06		−0.29		−.542	
Var. (APE)	4.39		30.18		14.86		15.99	
Autocorr.	−0.0727		−.1402		−0.310		−.21	

measures to protect industries may in some cases improve the employment performance. However, the results also show that protectionist policies are more likely to affect negatively the stock values and employment performance of protected industries. In fact, taken at face value, the results suggest that protectionist policies have failed to protect capital and employment in the economy as a whole.

NOTES

1. On this issue, see Jude Wannisky (1978) account of the Smoot-Hawley tariff act.
2. On this issue, see Pine (1984b).
3. See Greenhouse (1984a), story in the *New York Times*.
4. See Vinocur (1984).
5. See the *Wall Street Journal*, "EC's Retaliation on Steel Curbs Disappoints U.S."
6. See Martin (1984).
7. See the *New York Times*, "U.S. Trade Bar Angers Europeans."
8. See Lohr (1984).
9. See the *New York Times*, "Shoe-Import Quotas Asked."
10. See Greenhouse (1984b).
11. See Fialka (1984).
12. See the *Wall Street Journal*, "U.S.–Canada Talks Break Down on Treaty for Salmon Fishing."
13. See Lachica and Sieb (1984).
14. See the *Wall Street Journal*, "U.S. Tentatively Rules 3 Countries Subsidize Various Steel Exports."
15. See Farnsworth (1984a) and Carey (1984).
16. See Kilborn (1984).
17. See Ruback (1979).
18. See Brown and Warner (1983).
19. See Beaver (1981).
20. On this issue, see Christie (1983).
21. See Jain (1985) Ph.D. dissertation for a detailed discussion of the aggregation procedures.
22. Empirically we have defined a bull period as marked by a six-month continuous rise in a six-month moving average of the S&P 500.
23. The analysis was confined to restrictions affecting two and three digit SIC code industries. The reason is that in instances of trade actions affecting four, five or six digit industries, the collection of the relevant data proved to be very difficult.

7
The Trade Balance and Economic Activity

INTRODUCTION

The central tenet of much of the effort to improve the balance of trade of a particular country rests on the belief that a trade surplus is indicative of a healthy economy with rising income and employment. Considerable effort has been devoted by economists to analyze the determinants of a country's trade balance.

The relationship between U.S. economic growth and the U.S. trade balance can be better understood by viewing the economies of the United States and its trading partners as fully integrated in a single, global economy. From the perspective of the global economy, the relevant market is the *integrated* world market—not a collection of multiple markets in isolation. *Single* world market equilibrium prices and quantities will be determined by worldwide supply and demand conditions. *Global* equilibrium requires that there be only one worldwide price at which the supply of goods equals the demand for goods.

Given worldwide equilibrium and prices, local equilibrium in any specific country is not only unnecessary but highly improbable. Local disequilibria can be satisfied by trade in goods; excess supplies can be exported and excess demands satisfied by imports. In the global model, therefore, a trade balance surplus indicates that the local economy produced more goods than it consumed at going world prices. Conversely, a deficit in the balance of trade implies that the country demanded more goods than it supplied, at going world prices.

ALTERNATIVE APPROACHES TO
MODEL THE TRADE BALANCE

In general, most trade balance models fall into one of the following three approaches: elasticity, monetary, or absorption approach to the trade balance. The different approaches emphasize different aspects of the trade balance, thereby suggesting different variables to be included in any empirical model of a country's trade balance.

The Elasticity Approach

The elasticity approach focuses on an individual country's import and export functions. These functions are postulated as depending on the levels of national income and prices. Given the import and export price elasticities, one can determine whether changes in the terms of trade will result in an improvement in the country's trade balance.[1]

The elasticity approach has been criticized both on theoretical and empirical grounds.[2] One of the most comprehensive studies within this framework was undertaken by Houthakker and Magee (1969). Their study estimated elasticities of imports and exports on a commodity by commodity class. Invariably the Houthakker and Magee report estimated statistically significant income elasticities for the various import and export function. However, the price variable did not perform nearly as well. Many of the coefficients estimated were not statistically significant. This poor performance of the price elasticities may be due to the inadequacy of the import and export indexes.

An alternative way is to directly test the hypothesis that changes in policy variables that bring about changes in relative prices will result in changes in the trade balance. It is fairly apparent that, within the elasticity approach, policy variables such as trade restrictions or devaluation could affect either real incomes or the terms of trade and hence alter the trade balance.[3]

Import tariffs and export subsidies represent a set of policies commonly suggested when attempting to improve the balance of trade. Advocates of these policies observe that tariffs raise the domestic prices of imported goods and subsidies reduce the prices of exported products to foreigners (i.e., alter the terms of trade faced by domestic residents). This reduction in imports and the stimulus to exports are believed to improve the balance of trade and, consequently, domestic economic conditions.

However, proponents of free trade indicate that the real world effects of tariffs on the balance of trade are more complex. Their argument suggests that not only do tariffs reduce imports, but they are associated with a decline in exports as well (Figs. 7.1 and 7.2). Thus, the impact of tariffs on the trade balance is ambiguous (with the exception of the extreme case in which a country is running a trade balance deficit and then bans all imports). The decline in exports and imports indicates that the overall volume of trade is reduced by tariffs. Moreover, since both exports and imports are reduced by roughly the same amount, the effect of the tariff on the trade balance (exports less imports) will be negligible (Fig. 7.3). The regression results reported in Table 7.1 are consistent with these arguments.

These results can be understood by realizing that exports and imports are two sides of the same transaction: the object of producing goods for export is to be able to import and consume goods produced by foreigners. Producers and machines do not devote their work effort in order to acquire British pounds sterling and Japanese yen for their aesthetic appeal. The foreign currencies are exchanged for foreign goods to be imported

FIGURE 7.1. U.S. Imports and Tariff Rates, 1948–78.
(imports as a share of GNP vs. effective tariff rate)

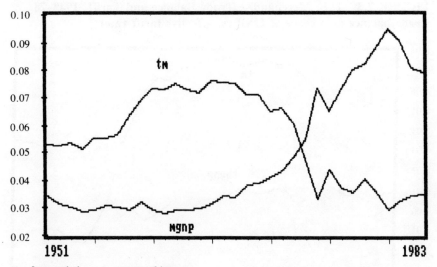

t_m—Import duties as a percent of imports
MGNP—Imports as a percent of GNP

Source: *National Income and Product Accounts of the United States*, U.S. Department of Commerce, Bureau of Economic Analysis.

FIGURE 7.2. U.S. Exports and Tariff Rates, 1948–78.
(exports as a share of GNP vs. effective tariff rate)

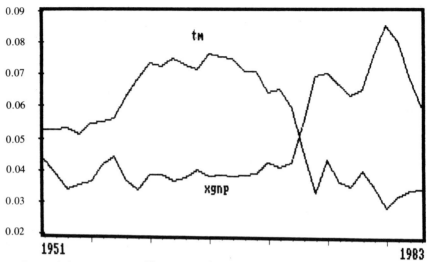

t_m—Import duties as a percent of imports
XGNP—Exports as a percent of GNP

    Source: National Income and Product Accounts of the United States, U.S. Department of Commerce, Bureau of Economic Analysis.

FIGURE 7.3. U.S. Merchandise Trade Balance and Tariff, 1948–78.
(trade balance as a share of GNP vs. effective tariff rate)

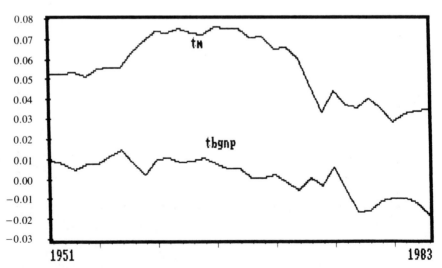

t_m—Import duties as a percent of imports
TBGNP—Trade balance as a percent of GNP

    Source: National Income and Product Accounts of the United States, U.S. Department of Commerce, Bureau of Economic Analysis.

TABLE 7.1. The Contemporaneous Relationship between the
Tariff Rates and Imports, Exports, and the Trade Balance (1951-83)

Dependent Variable	Constant	Independent Variable (Δtm)	R^2	D-W	S.E.	F
ΔM	.0009 (.0006)	−.704* (.119)	.528	1.77	.00355	34.69
ΔX	.000301 (.0008)	−.656* (.156)	.360	1.27	.0046	17.51
ΔTB	−.0006 (.0008)	.0482 (.164)	.002	2.09	.0048	.085

*Statistically significant at the 5% level.

or for foreign bonds, claims to future goods. The raison d'être for exporting is, per se, importing.

Suppose that a tariff successfully reduces the volume of imports by one-half. There are now only half as many foreign goods available to exchange for domestically produced goods, given the world terms of trade. So the volume of exports must be reduced symmetrically by one-half. The net effect on trade balance: None.

A tax on imports is equivalent in effect to a tax on exports. This principle is referred to as Lerner's Symmetry Theorem, a well-known principle of trade theory. Thus, the efficacy of protectionist measures to improve the trade balance is dubious on both theoretical and empirical grounds.

Trade restrictions, however, do reduce the efficiency of the world economy and reduce the standard of living of individuals in all trading partners. To the extent that trade restrictions are effective, the gains from trade in both production and consumption are lost. Production incentives shift away from those goods which are produced more efficiently domestically. Consumers are no longer able to choose goods produced more efficiently abroad. Trade restrictions devised to protect a particular industry may well accomplish that task for a period of time. But the cost of protecting that industry is borne by the rest of the economy.

The results of the causal relationship between the effective import rates, t_m, and the trade balance are reported in Table 7.2[4] The results fail to uncover any causal relationship between the trade balance and the effective import tax rates, although it is possible that the insignificance of the result may be due to the inadequacy of the effective tariffs rates, t_m. However, it is encouraging to note that the higher F statistics are consistent with the hypothesis that the trade balance causes trade restrictions,

TABLE 7.2. Granger Tests on the Causal Relationship between Tariff Rates, the Trade Balance, and Its Components

Dependent Variable	Explanatory Variable	$F(2,25)*$
Imports	t_m	1.68
Exports	t_m	1.33
Trade Balance	t_m	0.86
t_m	Imports	2.89
t_m	Exports	0.592
t_m	Trade Balance	2.61

*Critical value at 5% level is 3.38.

not the other way around. Similarly, the effective tax rates seem to have a higher predictive power on imports and exports than on the trade balance. These results are consistent with Lerner's Symmetry Theorem.

Historically, the effect of exchange rate and the trade balance has been analyzed in the context of a current devaluation. Advocates argue that a currency devaluation (i.e., depreciation in a floating rate system) will change the prices of goods in one country relative to another by changing the relationship in which prices in each currency are measured.

Advocates of devaluation observe that, following devaluation of the domestic currency, the price of foreign currencies, and therefore foreign-produced goods, will be higher for domestic citizens. At the same time, the price of the domestic currency, and therefore domestically-produced goods, will become lower for foreigners.

The rise in the price of imported goods will bring about a reduction in the level of imports, and the lower prices of goods exported to foreigners will increase the level of exports. With fewer imports and a stimulus to exports, the trade balance of the devaluing (depreciating currency) country will improve. Thus, devaluation (currency depreciation) should increase the competitiveness of an economy and improve its trade balance.

A study by Cooper (1971) lent support to those who argued for a devaluation of the dollar in 1971. Cooper's analysis of 24 devaluations effected by 19 countries during the 1959 to 1966 period showed that in 15 of the 24 episodes, an improvement in the balance of goods and services occurred in the year following devaluation.

Salant (1977) conducted a more extensive study of 101 devaluations by developed and less-developed countries. Of the 23 devaluations by developed countries, the trade balance improved in 8 instances and worsened in 15. Of the 78 LDC devaluations, the trade balance improved in 38 and worsened in 39 instances (staying unchanged in 1). In total, the balance of trade improved in 46 episodes of devaluation, worsened in 54, and did not change in 1. Salant's results indicate that, more often than not, devaluations lead to deterioration in the trade balance—not improvement.

The Salant study did not control for changes in other economic policy instruments. Miles (1979) conducted a study measuring the effects of devaluation after taking into account some of these factors. The other factors accounted for in his study were economic growth, monetary growth, and government spending. After accounting for these other factors, Miles found no evidence of devaluation improving the trade balance: a large negative effect on the trade balance was found in the year of devaluation and continued to have a net negative effect in the following three years, although a small positive effect was found in the year immediately following devaluation.

An explanation for the inability of a devaluation to improve the trade balance is that the economies of the United States and its trading partners are fully integrated into a single market. Imagine, for example, that after a 10 percent devaluation of the dollar, the price of wheat in Chicago falls 10 percent below the price of wheat in London. At that spread, trading companies would be willing to buy up the entire U.S. wheat crop. As a result, the price differential is dissipated almost immediately. What is true for wheat and other raw materials is equally true on average for all other goods and services in the economy. For example, after the price of wheat rises by 10 percent to reach equilibrium with the world price, the value of the land it is grown on can be expected to rise an equivalent amount. In this way, the change in the value of the basic commodity prices tends to permeate the entire price level. The net result is that the sought-after positive effects of devaluation (currency depreciation) are, in short order, fully offset by higher inflation in the devaluing country.

The Monetary Approach

The monetary approach has been used extensively in the analysis of the balance of payments of individual countries.[5] However, the literature pertaining to the monetary approach to the balance of trade is very limited. Nevertheless, the flow of goods has been analyzed within the context of the monetary approach.[6]

The monetary approach to the balance of payments focuses on the determinants of the excess domestic flow demand for or supply of money. The monetary approach to the balance of trade is based on the notion that the surplus or deficit in the currency account measures the extent to which the economy is accumulating claims on future income from abroad or vice versa. The accumulation or decumulation of these claims may take place either through international capital flows and/or money flows. Therefore, within this framework, monetary policy through its effect on the relative excess money supply could systematically affect the country's trade balance.

Results of the Granger tests on the causal relationship between the trade balance and money growth are reported in Table 7.3.[7] Upon inspection of the results reported in the table, it is apparent that the test fails to uncover any causal relationship between the money supply growth and the trade balance. This result combined with Miles, (1978) devaluation results lend support to the money neutrality hypothesis. Alternatively stated, the results suggest that nominal variables have no real impact on the trade balance.

The Absorption Approach

The absorption approach views the trade balance as a relation between expenditure and aggregate output (absorption) of the economy. The absorption approach focuses on the problems of adjustments in a way which highlights their policy implications. Its development can be traced to Alexander (1952) and Meade (1955) among others.

In general, policies designed to bring about changes in the current account can be classified into measures directed toward increasing output and measures aimed at reducing expenditure. Nevertheless, income and absorption are interdependent. Any changes in either income or expenditure will initiate changes in both of them. However, so long as the total increase in output is not offset by the change in aggregate demand the trade balance will improve.

It is apparent that traditional macroeconomic policy variables (e.g., government expenditures) will simultaneously affect the economy's net absorption. In addition to these policy variables, the authorities may also adopt commercial policies designed to switch expenditures away from imports into domestic goods and services.

The results in the Granger test on the causal relationship between government purchases of goods and services and the trade balance are

TABLE 7.3. Granger Tests on the Causal Relationship between Money Supply Growth and the Trade Balance

Dependent Variable	Explanatory Variable	$F*$
Trade Balance	Money Supply Growth	2.56 (2,28)
Money Supply Growth	Trade Balance	2.18 (2,28)

*Critical F at the 5% level is: $F(2,28)=3.34$.

reported in Table 7.4.[8] The test reported distinguished between defense and nondefense purchases of goods and services by the government. The reason for the distinction is that the perceived value of the services provided by the government as a result of these purchases may be different, therefore the increased purchases of defense and nondefense related services could generate different effects on the economy. The results reported in Table 7.4 uncover a causal relationship going from government purchases of nondefense goods and services to the trade balance and from the trade balance to real economic activity.[9] In short, the results reported in Table 7.4 are consistent with the view that increases in government purchases of goods and services increase the economy's excess demand for goods and services relative to the world, thereby resulting in a deterioration of the country's trade balance.

TABLE 7.4. The Causal Relationship between Government Purchases of Goods and Services and the Trade Balance: The Granger Tests

Dependent Variable	Explanatory Variable	F
Trade Balance	Defense Purchases	1.28 (2,33)
Trade Balance	Nondefense Purchases	4.48* (2,33)
Trade Balance	Real GNP Growth	2.25
Real GNP Growth	Trade Balance	3.76*

*Critical F at the 5% level is 3.30.

A TRADE BALANCE MODEL[10]

In order to capture as wide a spectrum of factor mobility as possible, factors of production are divided into those which are mobile (factor A) and those which are not (factor B).[11] The assumption that the world supply of each of the factors of production is exogenous at a point in time allows one to abstract from issues of capital accumulation or population growth. Nevertheless, the model allows for borrowing and lending between countries. However, since no capital accumulation takes place, the interest rate is determined by the rate of time preference of individual countries. Implicitly the presentation assumes a two-sector model where the preferences of the economic agents are assumed to be intertemporally separable.

The absence of capital accumulation suggests that the two factors of production may be viewed as different types of labor. With respect to the mobile factor, it is assumed that all forms of barriers, both natural and man-made, among the different states are absent. The mobile factor, therefore, is presumed to incur no costs when moving across state boundaries. Neither factor faces any moving costs within a country. The immobile factor, on the other hand, faces a prohibitive cost if moving across state boundaries is contemplated. Immobile factors of production must therefore be employed within the state where they are located. Following Becker (1965), the services emanating from the two factors are assumed to have two alternative uses. One is in the production of market goods and the other is in the production of a household (nonmarket) commodity.[12] Nonmarket production in one country need not be physically similar to nonmarket production in another country. Household (nonmarket) goods produced by the immobile factor, however, must be purchased and consumed in the country where that factor is located.

In order to keep the full separation between market and nonmarket activity, market and nonmarket goods must be imperfect substitutes both in demand and supply. There must, therefore, be either a unique factor in the production of the nonmarket good or some other characteristic of the production relation to ensure imperfect substitutability.[13]

For the purpose of this paper, we assume that each country produces a single market good using similar technology. The market good production process is assumed to be linear, homogenous, twice differentiable with both inputs indispensable, and is expressed as

(1) $\quad Y_i = F(N_{Ai}S_{Ai}, N_{Bi}S_{Bi})$

where N_{Ai} and N_{Bi} denote units of factors of production within each state and S_{Ai} and S_{Bi} denote utilization rates for each factor within the state. The utilization rate is normalized so that it is always between zero and unity. And Y_i denotes state i's production of market goods.

In the absence of man-made or natural barriers to trade (e.g., tariffs and transportation costs, respectively), arbitrage will ensure that the price of market goods will be the same in each country. Similarly, the mobility of factor A ensures that the reward to that factor, R_{Ai}, will be the same in all states. Finally, given common technology across states, it follows that the rewards to fixed factors may be equalized across countries.

In the presence of distorting tax rates, the necessary conditions for factor price equalization to obtain are fairly restrictive.[14] However, the pretesting of the different variables reported earlier did not uncover any direct linkage between tax rates and the trade balance. In what follows, the effect of distorting tax rates will be ignored. Alternatively stated, the model assumes that lump-sum neutral taxes are levied to finance the government purchases of goods and services. The neutral tax assumption leaves government purchases of goods and services as the only source of exogenous disturbances in the model.

The equalization of factor prices combined with the assumption of a similar linear, homogenous technology implies that the proportion of factor services used in the production of market goods in any state will be the same as that of the rest of the economy; that is,

$$\frac{N_{Ai}S_{Ai}}{N_{Bi}S_{Bi}} = \frac{N_{Aj}S_{Aj}}{N_{Bj}S_{Bj}} \quad \forall i,j \ldots$$

Thus, the ratio of output produced in a country to that of the world economy will be equal to the ratio of the immobile factor services supplied in the country relative to that of the total services supplied by the factor in the world economy;

(2) $\quad Y_i = \dfrac{N_{Bi}S_{Bi}}{H_{Bw}S_{Bw}} Y_w$

The next sections of the paper discuss the determination of the equilibrium levels of the supply of factors to the market sector and the overall production of market goods.

The Supply of Factor Services to the Market Sector

In this model, factor services can be employed in the production of market goods or in the production of the household commodity (nonmarket activity). The market-nonmarket decision is based, in part, on the opportunity cost of the factor's services. The operational measure of opportunities in this paper is the full income measure developed by Becker (1965). In addition to the value of the total endowment of services, factors of production will also include in their full income measure the actions of the government.[15] However, care must be exercised in the treatment of the effects of state and local government policies.

For simplicity and without loss of generality, it is assumed that if the factors of production do not pay any taxes, then they do not participate in the benefits provided by the revenues collected. Therefore, the actions of the local governments will not have any direct impact on the mobile factor, and any effect will be indirect insofar as the actions of the state government collectively have an effect on overall world prices. However, the actions of the local governments, in addition to the indirect effects described, will have a direct effect on the *immobile* factor insofar as the local government actions alter this factor's full income. All units of the immobile factor of production are assumed to be homogenous. As a result, local government services and taxes are distributed equally among the immobile factors of production within any country.

The analysis suggests that the utilization rate of the fixed factor will not necessarily be the same across countries. Consequently, the countries' output per unit of factor of production will differ insofar as the utilization rate of the fixed factor differs across state lines.[16]

In any country the mobile and immobile factors full income measure can be expressed as:

(3) $\quad \Omega_{Ai} = N_{Ai} R_A$

(4) $\quad \Omega_{Bi} = N_{Bi} R_B + \gamma G_i - T_i = N_{Bi} R_B + (\gamma - 1) G_i.$

where N_{Ai} denotes the country endowment of the mobile factor's services; G_i the government purchases of goods and services; T_i the local taxes;[17] and γ the value of the services provided by the government.[18]

Since the preferences are assumed to be intertemporally separable, the household demand for factors of production is postulated as depending on the factors' full income and the wage rate and interest rates as follows:

(5) $\qquad H_{Ai} = H_A[(\Omega_{Ai}/N_{Ai}), R_A, \varrho]$
$\qquad\qquad\qquad (+) \qquad (-)(-)$

(6) $\qquad H_{Bi} = H_B[(\Omega_{Bi}/N_{Bi}), R_B, \varrho]$
$\qquad\qquad\qquad (+) \qquad (-)(-)$

where Ω_{Ai}/N_{Ai} and Ω_{Bi}/N_{Bi} denote the full income of a unit of a factor of production, ϱ the interest rate. The signs of the first derivatives are indicated in parentheses below the right-hand side of the equation. The factor market equilibrium can be expressed as

(7) $\qquad S_{Ai} = 1 - H_{Ai}$

(8) $\qquad S_{Bi} = 1 - H_{Bi}$

The Aggregate Demand for Goods and Services

The per capita demand for market goods by each factor of production is postulated as depending on the factor's full income, the factor wage and interest rates and government purchases as follows:

(9) $\qquad AD_{Ai} = D_{Ai}(\dfrac{\Omega N_{Ai}}{N_{Ai}} , R_A, \varrho)$
$\qquad\qquad\qquad\quad (+) \quad (+)(-)$

(10) $\qquad AD_{Bi} = D_{Bi}(\dfrac{\Omega_{Bi}}{N_{Bi}} , R_B, \varrho) - \gamma G_i$
$\qquad\qquad\qquad\quad (+) \quad (+)(-)$

where the sign under the variables denotes the sign of the partial derivative. Notice also that the specification explicitly assumes that government purchases have no direct effect on the mobile factor demand for goods and services. On the other hand, in addition to having a direct effect on the immobile factor income, government services also have a direct impact on the private sector purchases of goods and services. That is, given a positive value, the government provisions of goods and services will result in a reduction in private sector purchases.

Combining equations 2 and 3 with the government purchases of goods and services yields an expression for the economy's aggregate demand.

$$(11) \quad AD_i = D_{Ai} + D_{Bi} + (1 - \gamma)G_i$$

The world demand for goods and services is easily derived by adding each country's aggregate demand. That is,

$$(12) \quad AD_w = \Sigma AD_i$$

The assumption that the mobile factor does not consume any of the government services, and that the value of the government services, γ, is the same across countries allows one to aggregate some of the world demand for goods and services as follows:

$$(12') \quad AD_w = D_{Aw} + \Sigma D_{Bi} + (1 - \gamma)G_w$$

Worldwide equilibrium requires the equation of the world demand and world supply of goods and services. That is,

$$(13) \quad AD_w = Y_w$$

In equilibrium the demand for the various factors of production will be equated to their supply. However, full employment of the factors of production (equations 7 and 8) does not necessarily guarantee that the domestic production of market goods (equation 2) will equal the domestic demand (equation 11). The difference between the two quantities will determine the economy's net trade position. That is,

$$(14) \quad TB_i = Y_i - AD_i$$

A positive trade balance implies an accumulation of assets (positive savings) to be depleted (consumed) in the following period.

Country-Specific Equilibrium: The Trade Balance

A simple interpretation can be provided for the model developed in this paper. Within an integrated economy framework, two separate types of equilibria are of interest. The first is country-specific equilibrium, that is, the equation of the demand and supply of goods and services and for factors of production within a given country. The second is overall equilibrium, that is, the equation of total demand and supply of goods and factors of production within the world economy. The first type of equilibrium may be achieved through a redistribution of goods and the mobile factor of production among countries. If a country is assumed to be small relative to the world economy, it will face given terms of trade (i.e., given gross-of-tax relative prices). Given the relative price and public spending and tax rates, the utilization rate for each factor of production will be determinate; thus, any change in supply of factor services must occur through a change in the country endowment. Similarly, the demand per unit of factor of production will be determinate; thus, any imbalance in the goods market must necessarily occur through a net export or import from other countries.

That is, if the demand for goods and/or factors of production does not initially equal the supply of goods or factors of production within the country then the incipient excess demand or supply will generate a tendency for the relative prices in the state to change. However, the potential for arbitrage (through trade in goods or mobile factor migration) will dissipate any incipient change in relative prices. In the absence of interstellar trade, such quantity redistributions will not necessarily achieve total equilibrium, since such flows only eliminate relative excess demand and supplies across states and, consequently, will not eliminate a worldwide excess demand or excess supply. Aggregate excess demand may require an adjustment in the economy's relative prices in order to bring about overall equilibrium in all markets.

The important point is simply that since prices are equalized across countries, a change in relative prices will tend to have the same proportionate effect in all countries. Thus, part of the change in economic activity attributable to the relative price change will generate a component common to all states and, to a large extent, this component will be exogenous to the state government. However, to the extent that governments can influence the full income of the fixed factor, the utilization rate, and then the total services supplied by the fixed factor, can be influenced by state spending. As a result, output per unit factor of production may differ across countries.

THE EFFECT OF FISCAL POLICY ON THE RELATIONSHIP BETWEEN THE TRADE BALANCE AND ECONOMIC ACTIVITY

The previous section illustrated how the basic model developed in this paper focuses on two types of equilibria: one being the equation of total demand and supply of goods and factors of production within the world economy, the other being the equation of the demand for and supply of goods and factors of production within a given country. The latter equilibrium is of particular interest to this section, because country-specific equilibrium is achieved through a redistribution of goods and factors of production across countries. Hence, focusing on the country-specific equilibrium allows one to analyze the effect of fiscal policy on the relationship between the trade balance and economy activity.

The integrated economy framework postulates that in equilibrium, changes in quantity movements (i.e., the trade balance) will be the direct result of changes in the country's relative excess demand for goods. The effect of government purchases of goods and services on a country's economic performance relative to the world can be shown to be:[19]

$$(15) \quad EY_i - EY_w = \left(\frac{H_B}{1 - H_B} \right) \left(\frac{N_B}{1 - H_B} \right)$$
$$\eta_{B\Omega}(1 - \gamma) \left(\frac{dG_i}{N_{Bi}} - \frac{dG_w}{N_{Bw}} \right)$$

where $\eta_{B\Omega}$ denotes the income elasticity of demand for household time.

Similarly, the effect of government purchases on the trade balance can be shown to be:

$$(16) \quad \frac{d(TB_i)}{Y_i} = -\left\{ \left(\frac{H_B}{1 - H_B} \right) \left(\frac{N_B}{\Omega_B} \right) \eta_{BR} + \left(\frac{D_B}{AD} \right) \left(\frac{\epsilon_{B\Omega}}{\Omega_B} \right) N_B + \frac{N_B}{AD} \right\} (1 - \gamma) \left(\frac{dG_{Ni}}{NB_i} - \frac{dG_w}{NB_w} \right)$$

where η_{BR} denotes the magnitude of the household elasticity of demand for leisure with respect to the real wage rate.

The relationship between a country's trade balance and real economic performance induced by changes in government purchases of goods and services is easily derived combining equations 15 and 16.

$$(17) \quad \frac{d(TB_i)}{Y_i} = -$$
$$\left\{ \frac{\left(\frac{H_B}{1 - H_B} \right) \left(\frac{N_B}{\Omega_B} \right) \eta_{BR} + \left(\frac{N_B}{AD} \right) \left[1 + \left(\frac{D_B}{\Omega_B} \right) \epsilon_{B\Omega} \right]}{\left(\frac{H_B}{1 - H_B} \right) \left(\frac{N_B}{\Omega_B} \right) \eta_{B\Omega}} \right\} (EY_i - EY_w)$$

Upon inspection of equations 15, 16, and 17, it is apparent that the effect of government expenditures in economic activity and the trade balance will depend critically on the perceived value of government provided services, (i.e., γ). If the value of the government services is worth less than the cost of producing the public services ($\gamma < 1$), an increase in government purchases will simultaneously result in the following:

1. An increase in the economy's aggregate demand relative to the world economy.
2. A reduction in the economy's full income which will result in a reduction of leisure consumption, thereby increasing market employment and production relative to the world economy.

Since the information accumulated in the assumed relationship allows us to establish that the relative increase in aggregate demand will be larger than the relative increase in aggregate supply, we see that the trade balance will unambiguously worsen as economic activity increases. Thus the model developed in this paper suggests that changes in government purchases of goods and services will induce a negative relationship between the trade balance and economic activity.

THE TRADE BALANCE AND ECONOMIC ACTIVITY: THE EVIDENCE

A stochastic version of equation (17) is now used to estimate the relationship between trade balance and economic activity. That is,

$$\frac{\Delta TB_i}{Y_i} = \alpha_0 - \alpha_1(EY_i - EY_w) + \mu$$

where ΔTB is calculated as changes in the merchandise trade balance, in constant dollars. Real GNP is used as a measure of the countries' levels of economic activity (i.e., Y_i). The world real income (Y_w) is approximated by the sum of the real incomes of the countries included in the analysis.

The relationship between the trade balance and economic growth was analyzed for the U.S., Japan, and nine European countries (Austria, Denmark, Germany, Italy, Netherlands, Spain, Sweden, Switzerland, and the United Kingdom). The results are reported in Table 7.5. Nine of the eleven countries exhibited a negative and statistically significant relation-

TABLE 7.5. Estimates of the Relationship between the Trade Balance and Economic Activity

Dependent Variable (DTB/Y)	Constant	Independent Variables				D-W	R^2	S.E.	F_l
		$(EY_i - EY_w)$	AR(1)	D49	D				
Austria	-.00164 (.00238)	-.151 (.045)				2.04	.306	.012	11.02
Denmark	.00511 (.0055)	-.0348 (.010)				1.45	.327	.0285	12.17
Germany	.0019 (.0018)	-.0088 (.0287)				1.80	.0037	.0093	.093
Italy	.00196 (.00338)	-.120 (.061)				2.51	.131	.0174	3.77
Japan	.00779 (.0021)	-.0572 (.0291)	-.453 (.184)	-.030 (.007)		2.08	.431	.0094	5.57
Netherlands	.0039 (.0029)	-.108 (.049)				1.68	.159	.0152	4.74
Spain	-.00184 (.0025)	-.096 (.024)				2.17	.380	.0133	15.37
Sweden	.0007 (.0016)	-.0827 (.0314)	-.482 (.186)			2.16	.327	.0121	5.60
Switzerland	.0016 (.0029)	-.072 (.047)			-.049 (.015)	1.72	.306	.015	5.31
UK	-.0097 (0.14)	.100 (.141)				1.99	.019	.073	.508
U.S.	-.00162 (.001)	-.053 (.031)				1.97	.103	.0048	2.89

ship between their relative growth rates and their trade balances—the exceptions being the UK, with a positive coefficient, and Germany, with a negative coefficient.[20]

As expected, the evidence suggests that more often than not trade deficits or a deterioration of the trade balance is associated with a healthy, growing economy demanding resources from the rest of the world. However, this relationship should not be interpreted as a "causal" one. The theoretical model developed in the previous section suggests that the negative correlation between the trade balance and the country's growth rate relative to the world may be the result of fiscal policy shocks.

CONCLUSIONS

The trade account can be viewed as the means by which an aggregate economy can adjust its temporal pattern of consumption and investment, on the one hand, and production and savings, on the other hand. During most of the nation's first century, for example, the investment opportunities in the United States exceeded the domestic economy's aggregate savings. Stated differently, during this period, more goods and services (consumption) and capital goods (investment) were acquired than were produced. The difference was the net imports from the rest of the world, as foreign suppliers provided the excess goods, services, and capital goods, in exchange for future claims (bonds and stocks) against the output of the U.S. economy. Conversely, in the 1950s, investment opportunities in rebuilding Europe and Japan exceeded those economies' savings and production relative to their consumption. The U.S. ran a trade balance surplus and invested heavily in foreign nations.

NOTES

1. An exhaustive survey of this literature can be found in Magee (1975).

2. For a discussion of the main empirical problems associated with the estimation of the elasticities see Orcutt (1950).

3. Granger (1969) suggests a simple way to analyze the causal relationship between the trade balance and any other variable. The Granger test is based on the premise that if forecast of the trade balance obtained using both post values of the trade balance and another variable are better than the forecasts obtained using values of the trade balance alone, then the variable in question is said to "cause" the trade balance.

4. See Appendix A for a discussion of the sample data and the estimated equations used in calculating the F statistics used in the Granger test.

5. For a collection of papers on the theoretical and empirical issues on the monetary approach to the balance of payments see Frenkel and Johnson (1976).

6. See Craig (1981).

7. See Appendix B for a discussion of the sample, the data, and the regression results from which the Granger tests were calculated.

8. See Appendix C for a discussion of the variables, sample, and regression results on which the tests are based.

9. A causal relationship going from the trade balance to government purchases of goods and services was not investigated.

10. The model developed in this section draws heavily on Canto and Webb (1983).

11. For simplicity of exposition, factors are classified as either mobile or fixed. In principle, the analysis could also be extended to allow for differing degrees of factor mobility (i.e., adjustment costs). For a two-sector model with adjustment costs see Mussa (1978).

12. The household commodity is assumed to be produced by the following linear homogenous, twice-differentiable production function:

$$Z = f(H,X)$$

where H denotes the amount of household time (i.e., leisure) and X the amount of market goods used in the production process. The cost of the household commodity for each factor in a given state i can be written as

$$\Pi_{Ai} = \Pi(R^*_{Ai}, 1)$$

$$\Pi_{Bi} = \Pi(R^*_{Bi}, 1)$$

where the price of the market good is the numeraire, and R^*_{Ai} and R^*_{Bi} denote the real after tax factor return (that is, the opportunity cost of leisure in terms of market goods).

13. The assumption that the nonmarket commodity is produced and consumed in the household guarantees the imperfect substitutability conditions described.

14. The general conditions under which trade is sufficient to equalize factor returns are well known in the literature (see Samuelson [1949]). The effects of factor migration and factor price equalization are also well known (see Mundell [1957]).

In our model factor price equalization can be easily shown as follows: First, free trade assures that the price of the market good is equalized across countries. Second, the price of the market good can be decomposed into the weighted sum of each factor's proportionate share of production costs times its respective *before tax* factor payments, or

$$P = \alpha R_{Ai} + (1 - \alpha)R_{Bi}$$

The above equation may be set equal to 1 since the market good is also the numeraire. Similarly, the average production cost for the mobile factor's household commodity can be written as

$$\Pi_{Ai} = \theta R^*_{Ai} + (1 - 0)$$

where θ denotes the share of leisure in the production of the household good. Third, if one assumes that state and local tax revenues are distributed only to the fixed factor, this guarantees that the mobile factor's full income is independent of its locality. Thus minimizing Π_A will, in fact, be equivalent to maximizing the utility of the mobile factor since such actions will maximize household consumption (Z_A), which is the only argument in the factor of production utility function. Consequently, the mobile factor will migrate to the country with the lowest Π_A. If mobile factors reside in all countries this implies that

$$\Pi_A = \Pi_{Ai} \;\forall\; i$$

Since the household good is not taxed (although the market goods input is), it follows that

$$R^*_{Ai} = R^*_{Aj}$$

which is the result that the mobile factor will be taxed at the same rate in every state.

The gross of tax relative factor cost in market production (R_{Ai}/R_{Bi}) and the tax rate on the mobile factor can be expressed in terms of the relative prices (R^*_A/P) and (R^*_A/Π_A): Differentiating logarithmically the two relative prices and solving for (R_{Ai}/R_{Bi}) and t_{Ai} yields

$$E\frac{R_{Ai}}{R_{Bi}} = \frac{(1-\theta)E(P/\Pi_A) + \theta E(R^*_A/\Pi_A)}{\theta}$$

$$t_{Ai} = -\frac{(1-\alpha)\theta E(R^*_A/\Pi_A) + (1-(1-\alpha)(1-\theta))E(P/\Pi_A)}{\theta}$$

where E denotes the $d$log operator.

Using this result and the market good equation yield $R_{Bi} = R_{Bj}$, even though $R^*_{Bi} \neq R^*_{Bj}$.

15. Since by assumption there is no unemployment of either factor of production (i.e., they are always engaged in either market or nonmarket activity), the market reward to each factor of production represents the appropriate measure to value the factor services—both market and nonmarket.

16. Since by assumption the before- and after-tax rates are equalized across countries, the only variable left to generate a differential factor utilization rate across countries is the income effect generated by changes in government purchases of goods and services.

17. The assumption of a balanced budget implies that $G_i = T_i$ at all times.

18. Conventional accounting techniques value government services at factor costs. However, there is no reason why the value of these services should equal their costs, as pointed out by Bailey (1971). Thus, in any analysis of fiscal policy, a provision should be made for this possibility. The above formulation implicitly assumes that the value of the government services provided by state or federal government services is the same.

19. Notice that the formulation assumes that the mobile and immobile factors have the same marginal propensities. See Appendix B for a formal derivation of the results.

20. D_{49} is a $(0,1)$ dummy variable intended to capture the 1974, 1979, oil shocks. D is a dummy variable intended to capture the 1974 oil shock.

APPENDIX A: GRANGER TESTS ON THE RELATIONSHIP BETWEEN EFFECTIVE TARIFF RATE, THE TRADE BALANCE, IMPORTS, AND EXPORTS

Information on the U.S. trade balance, imports, exports, and tariff revenues was obtained from the national income and product account tables. Information on the consumer price index was obtained from the economic report of the president.

The variables used in the various regressions are defined as follows:

M = U.S. imports deflated by the U.S. CPI and U.S. GNP
X = U.S. exports deflated by the U.S. CPI and U.S. GNP
TB = The U.S. trade balance deflated by the U.S. CPI and U.S. GNP
T_m = Tariff revenues divided by the value of imports

The Granger test requires that the data exhibit stationarity. Therefore, where appropriate, the series have been differenced. Diagnostic checks on the residuals of the estimated equations failed to uncover any nonstationarity in the data. The estimated equations were of the following form.

$$Y_t = C + a_1 Y_{t-1} + a_2 Y_{t-2} + b_1 Z_{t-1} + b_2 Z_{t-2} + \epsilon$$

The significance of lagged value of Z given lagged values of Y is tested as a restriction on the equation. The F statistics corresponding to such a test are reported in the text.

TABLE A.1. Regression Results: The Granger Tests

Dependent Variable	Independent Variable	Constant	a_1	a_2	b_1	b_2	R^2	D-W	SSR
ΔM	—	.00145 (.00111)	-.015 (.19)	.077 (.20)	—	—	.005	2.03	.000801
ΔM	Δl_m	.00116 (.00114)	-.232 (.281)	.450 (.326)	-.411 (.275)	.369 (.291)	.123	1.99	.000706
ΔX	—	.0010 (.0007)	.686 (.150)	-.678 (.163)	—	—	.505	1.92	.000469
ΔX	Δl_m	.0011 (.0007)	.728 (.190)	-.875 (.201)	.083 (.180)	-.283 (.180)	.553	2.02	.000424
ΔTB	—	-.06104 (.0008)	-.164 (.186)	-.318 (.186)	—	—	.110	2.04	.000621
ΔTB	Δl_m	-.00121 (.0009)	-.148 (.189)	-.381 (.194)	-.223 (.170)	.0009 (.168)	.168	2.01	.000581
Δl_m	—	-.00056 (.001)	.081 (.192)	-.0116 (.193)	—	—	.006	1.98	.000861
Δl_m	ΔM	-.0002 (.0011)	.504 (.274)	-.387 (.290)	.444 (.280)	-.599 (.324)	.194	1.91	.000699
Δl_m	X	-.0007 (.001)	-.012 (.250)	0.114 (.252)	-.178 (.265)	.287 (.280)	.052	1.99	.000822
Δl_m	ΔTB	-.0005 (.001)	.201 (.187)	-.094 (.184)	-.278 (.208)	.398 (.213)	.192	1.98	.000700

APPENDIX B: GRANGER TESTS ON THE CAUSAL RELATIONSHIP BETWEEN MONEY SUPPLY GROWTH AND THE TRADE BALANCE

Information on the U.S. money supply (M_1) was obtained from the bank and monetary statistics series published by the Board of Governors of the Federal Reserve system.

The variables used in the regression were defined as follows:

TB = The U.S. trade balance deflated by the U.S. CPI and U.S. GNP

M_1 = The percent change in the U.S. money supply (M_1)

TABLE B.1. Regression Results: The Granger Tests

Dependent Variable	Independent Variable	Constant	a_1	a_2	b_1	b_2	R^2	D-W	SSR
TB	—	-.000754 (.00088)	.781 (.167)	.169 (.162)	—	—	.731	1.87	.000705
TB	M_1	.0036 (.0032)	.565 (.193)	.191 (.171)	-.108 (.048)	.018 (.051)	.771	1.80	.000599
M_1	—	.013 (.007)	.616 (.176)	.126 (.174)	—	—	.445	2.12	.01214
M_1	TB	.036 (.013)	.400 (.205)	-.124 (.216)	-1.10 (.812)	-.454 (.718)	.517	2.02	.01055

APPENDIX C: THE CAUSAL RELATIONSHIP BETWEEN GOVERNMENT PURCHASES OF GOODS AND SERVICES AND THE TRADE BALANCE

Information on U.S. defense and nondefense government purchases of goods and services was obtained from the survey of current business. Information on the U.S. population was obtained from the U.S. Bureau of Census (series P-25).

The variables used in the regressions are defined as follows:

TB = The U.S. trade balance deflated by the U.S. CPI and U.S. GNP

DFR = U.S. government purchases of defense-related goods and services deflated by the U.S. CPI and U.S. population

$NDFR$ = U.S. government purchases of nondefense-related goods and services deflated by the U.S. CPI and U.S. population

EY = The percent change in real GNP

TABLE C.1. Regression Results: The Granger Tests

Dependent Variable	Independent Variable	Constant	a_1	a_2	b_1	b_2	R^2	D-W	SSR
TB	—	-.00087 (.0009)	.718 (.184)	.114 (.178)	—	—	.658	1.71	.000900
TB	DFR	-.0073 (.004)	.638 (.180)	.217 (.154)	.0000028 (.000028)	.000028 (.000025)	.724	1.95	.000827
TB	NDFR	.0011 (.0046)	.431 (.187)	.104 (.133)	-.00015 (.00009)	.000019 (.0001)	.771	1.80	.000689
TB	EY	-.0039 (.001)	.727 (.190)	.024 (.189)	.061 (2.90)	.041 (.029)	.729	1.80	.000711
EY	—	.033 (.009)	.074 (.177)	-.092 (.184)	—	—	.012	1.80	.0355
EY	TB	.038 (.009)	-.148 (.171)	-.071 (.172)	-.626 (1.12)	2.61 (1.11)	3.14	2.18	.0246

APPENDIX D: THE EFFECTS OF FISCAL POLICY ON THE RELATIONSHIP BETWEEN THE TRADE BALANCE AND ECONOMIC ACTIVITY

In order to solve for the effect of changes in government purchases on the trade balance, one may choose to focus first on the following components:

1. The effect of government purchases of goods and services on the country's supply of market goods relative to the world supply.
2. The effect of government purchases on the country's aggregate demand for market goods relative to the world demand.

The next step in the analysis is to derive an expression for the two components of the relative excess demand. Differentiating logarithmically, equation 2 yields

$$(A.1) \qquad EY_i = ES_{Bi} - ES_{Bw} + EY_w$$

where E denotes the $d$log operator.

Similarly, differentiating logarithmically the demand for nonmarket services, equation 6 yields

$$(A.2) \qquad EH_{Bi} = \eta_{B\Omega i}\left(\frac{R_B N_{Bi}}{\Omega_{Bi}}\right)ER_B + \frac{(\gamma - 1)}{\Omega_{Bi}}\,dG_i - \eta_{BR}ER_B - \eta_{BP}E\varrho$$

where $\eta_{B\Omega i}$ denotes the income elasticity of demand for household item services, η_{BR} the household demand elasticity with respect to the factor's wage rate, and η_{BP} the household demand elasticity with respect to the interest rate.

Differentiating the factor market equilibrium condition, equation 8 yields

$$(A.3) \qquad ES_{Bi} = -\frac{H_{Bi}}{(1 - H_{Bi})}EH_{Bi}$$

In what follows in order to simplify the presentation, the full income semielasticity, the household's own price elasticity of demand for household time, and the interest rate elasticity of demand for household time are assumed to be identical across countries, that is:

(A.4) $\quad \dfrac{N_{Bi}}{\Omega_{Bi}}\eta_{B\Omega i}=\dfrac{N_{Bj}}{\Omega_{Bj}}\eta_{B\Omega J},\forall\; i,j\ldots$

(A.5) $\quad \eta_{BRi}=\eta_{BRj} \qquad \forall\; i,j\ldots$

and

(A.6) $\quad \eta_{B\varrho i}=\eta_{B\varrho j} \qquad \forall\; i,j\ldots$

Substituting equations A.2, A.3, A.4, A.5, and A.6 into equation A.1 yields, after some manipulation, the following expression for the effect of government purchases on the country's supply of goods and services relative to the rest of the world.

(A.7) $\quad EY_i-EY_w=\left(\dfrac{H_B}{1-H_B}\right)\left(\dfrac{N_B}{\Omega_B}\right)\eta_{B\Omega}(1-\gamma)\left(\dfrac{dG_i}{N_{Bi}}-\dfrac{dG_w}{H_{Bw}}\right)$

Differentiating logarithmically equations 11 and 12 one obtains:

(A.8) $\quad EAD_i=\dfrac{D_{Ai}}{AD_i}ED_{Ai}+\dfrac{D_{Bi}}{AD_i}ED_{Bi}+\dfrac{(1-\gamma)}{AD_i}dG_i$

(A.9) $\quad EAD_w=\dfrac{D_{Aw}}{AD_w}ED_{Aw}+\dfrac{D_{Bw}}{AD_w}ED_{Bw}+\dfrac{(1-\gamma)}{AD_w}dG_w$

Again assuming similar elasticities and starting from a situation where all the governments behave identically

(A.10) $\quad \dfrac{Gi}{N_{Bi}}=\dfrac{Gw}{N_{Bw}}$

the expression for the effect of government purchases on the country's aggregate demand relative to the world demand simplifies to

(A.11) $\quad EAD_i-EAD_w=\dfrac{DB}{AD}\left(\dfrac{\epsilon_{B\Omega}N_B}{\Omega}\right)$

$$+\left(\dfrac{N_B}{AD}\right)(1-\gamma)\left(\dfrac{dG_i}{N_{Bi}}-\dfrac{dG_w}{N_{Bw}}\right)$$

Keeping in mind that worldwide equilibrium requires $(EY_w = EAD_i)$, subtracting equations A.7 from A.8 yields

$$(A.12) \quad EAD_i - EY_i = \left\{ \left(\frac{H_B}{1-H_B} \right) \frac{N_B}{\Omega_B} \eta_{BR} + \frac{D_B}{AD} + \frac{\epsilon_{B\Omega}}{\Omega} N_B \right.$$

$$\left. + \frac{N_B}{AD} \right\} (1-\gamma) \left(\frac{dG_{Ni}}{N_{Bi}} - \frac{dG_w}{NB_w} \right)$$

If as previously assumed, initially all governments behave in identical fashion, countries will necessarily have balanced trade. Hence, equation 16 may be expressed as

$$(A.13) \quad \frac{d(TB_i)}{Y_i} = -\left\{ \left(\frac{H_B}{1-H_B} \right) \left(\frac{N_B}{\Omega_B} \right) \eta_{BR} + \left(\frac{D_B}{AD} \right) \left(\frac{\epsilon_{B\Omega}}{\Omega_B} \right) N_B \right.$$

$$\left. + \frac{N_B}{AD} \right\} (1-\gamma) \left(\frac{dG_{Ni}}{N_{Bi}} - \frac{dG_w}{NB_w} \right)$$

Equation A.13 describes the effect of government purchases on the trade balance. Substituting equation A.7 into A.13, one obtains an expression for the relationship between the trade balance and economic activity resulting from government purchases of goods and services.

$$(A.14) \quad \frac{d(TB_i)}{Y_i} = -$$

$$\left\{ \frac{\left(\frac{H_B}{1-H_B} \right) \left(\frac{N_B}{\Omega_B} \right) \eta_{BR} + \left(\frac{N_B}{AD} \right) \left(1 + \frac{D_B}{\Omega_B} \epsilon_{B\Omega} \right)}{\left(\frac{H_B}{1-H_B} \right) \left(\frac{N_B}{\Omega_B} \right) \eta_{B\Omega}} \right\} (EY_i - EY_w)$$

8
U.S. Trade Policy: An Interpretation

INTRODUCTION

Errant trade policy constitutes a big threat to the outlook for above average performance by the U.S. economy for the remainder of the decade. The gradual shift towards a bilateral "fair" trade as opposed to "free" trade is very divisive. The rhetoric utilized in the arguments favoring "fair" trade quickly evolves into a bilateral "us versus them," them being Japan, Europe or some developing nation.

The steady drift towards an increasing protectionism on the part of different U.S. administrations demonstrates their willingness to risk substantial retaliations by the U.S. trading partners—thereby damaging some sectors of the economy—in order to show they can "play tough" when it comes to trade. Politically, these policies enjoy considerable support among different domestic groups. This, perhaps more than anything else, may explain the popularity of the "get tough" attitude by the administration.

Theoretically, these actions may benefit only a sector of the economy; more often than not the trade actions may impose some costs on the rest of the economy. To the extent that it is sufficiently costly on the rest of the economy to get together, the special interest groups will be successful in obtaining the protectionist legislation. Trade actions resulting from the activities of special interest groups have been classified in this book as microevents. In contrast, trade actions resulting from and/or affecting significantly the majority of sectors in the economy have been classified as macroevents.

The Trade Act of 1974 provides the vehicle by which the special interest groups' demands may be satisfied. In addressing problems created by import competition that is considered "fair," the Trade Act of 1974 provides that an industry no longer needs to demonstrate that its injury was caused by imports resulting from an earlier tariff concession or that imports are the "major" cause, i.e., a cause no less important than any other cause, of its injury.

The steel industry is a classic case that illustrates the power of special interest groups and responsiveness of politicians to their demands. In spite of the historical record, during the 1984 presidential campaign the ITC recommended trade restriction in the import of steel. Democratic presidential nominee Walter Mondale had already actively campaigned for protecting the domestic steel industry. On the face of it, the political considerations seemed to dictate doing "something" to protect the steel industry. Thirty-six states produce steel and the nine largest producers— Indiana, Ohio, Pennsylvania, Michigan, Illinois, Kentucky, New York, California and Texas—have a total of 225 electoral votes (See Farnsworth (1984a)).

Upon closer inspection, it was far from clear that moving to co-opt Mondale on the trade issue would enhance Reagan's or the Republicans' chances for victory in November. In the primary campaign, for example, Gary Hart explicitly rejected the call for protectionism, saying it would cost more jobs than it would save. Hart, against great odds, nearly matched Mondale in the popular vote. The president, his administration and the Republican Party were perfectly positioned to reject the ITC's recommendation. The President, at least rhetorically, has always been a strong advocate of free trade. In addition, the steel industry itself was in an upswing, thanks to the general recovery. Through the first week of July, steel production for the year was up 27.6 percent from its year earlier figures. Production through July 1984 used 75.8 percent of the industry's capacity, up from 53.2 percent of a year earlier. Employment too, had showed definite signs of recovery. Steel employment in May climbed to 181,174, 7.2 percent above its 1983 low of 168,853. There have been few such propitious moments to draw the line on further trade restrictions. However, in September 1984, the administration decided to seek worldwide voluntary restraints on steel imports. This decision and its unilateral embargoes on European imports of pipe and tube steel demonstrate the administration's willingness to risk substantial retaliation by its largest trading partners—and thereby, damage to other parts of the economy—in order to show it can "play tough" when it comes to industry-specific policies.

THE NATURE OF PROTECTIONIST POLICIES

The potential benefits to be derived from protectionism lead to the formation of special interest groups. The nature of the protectionist policies implemented depend in part on the demands of the special interest groups, as well as the possible costs imposed on the domestic economy and on the rest of the world. In turn, the response by the rest of the world depends in part on the nature of the U.S. restrictions. Under the GATT escape clause, individual countries are allowed, under certain circumstances, to protect domestic industries through tariffs without any serious retribution by the rest of the world. Further protective measures may also be allowed provided that individual countries consult with each other when trade problems arise. Whether violations of international arrangements (GATT) occur depends on the rest of the world's ability to retaliate and/or enforce the GATT agreements. As before, in discussing the nature of trade actions, we argued that the distinction between macro (across-the-board) and micro (industry-specific) trade policy proves to be a significant one.

The Case For Protection Through Tariffs

The nature of the macrorestrictions imposed by the U.S. has to a large extent followed the GATT guidelines. One possible explanation for this behavior is that politically and economically it represents the least costly alternative. In fact, a strong argument can be made that tariffs represent the least expensive way to provide a given degree of protection to the domestic economy. That is, if the objective of the policy is to maintain a percentage differential between the domestic and foreign prices, tariffs are the most efficient way to do it. Given the assumption that some trade will occur, this differential remains unaltered in the presence of domestic and/or foreign demand and supply shocks. On the other hand, imposition of quotas implies that the differential between domestic and foreign prices will vary with demand and/or supply shocks. In conclusion, if a given degree of protection is desired, the quota will require continuous adjustment to market conditions. This logic suggests that at the macro-level where the emphasis is not so much on preserving a given number of jobs, but on preserving a given standard of living (i.e., salary and rates of returns) for the domestic residents, tariffs are the desired instrument to carry out across-the-board protectionist policies. Furthermore, as the standard of living of domestic citizens increases, the need for across-the-board protectionist policies declines. To the extent that the reductions in across-the-board restriction increase the efficiency of the world economy, the standard of living of both the U.S. and the rest of the world will increase. This line of reasoning provides, in part, an explanation for U.S. macro trade policy during the post-war period up to the late 1960s when the U.S. economy experienced a significant expansion. U.S. macro trade policy was one of advocating across-the-board trade restriction. It also explains the gradual shift towards what may be considered major trade restrictions in the 1970s and 1980s, a period in which the U.S. economic performance deteriorated.

The U.S. influence is also felt in other countries' trade policies. Throughout the 1960s and 1970s, in the face of possible U.S. actions, Japan made numerous trade concessions. However, the reduction and/or elimination of trade restrictions occurred mostly in industries in which Japan was gaining a comparative advantage. Nevertheless it is worthwhile to point out that the behavior of both the U.S. and Japan is consistent with the view that macro trade actions are aimed at preserving the standard of living of large segments of the population and that the most efficient way to achieve this protection is through tarriffs (price restrictions).

The Case For Protection Through Quotas

Micro trade policies are aimed at maintaining the standard of living of particular interest groups. The benefits of the micro trade policies are usually concentrated in a small segment of the population (i.e., an industry), while the costs of the action are generally spread out over the rest of the domestic economy and, in some instances the rest of the world. The protectionist policies usually are enacted to give the troubled industry some breathing room while it adjusts to the new market conditions. The objective of the policies is to ease the transition to a new equilibrium. In some cases more permanent measures are taken to guarantee survival, and hence some minimum employment level, in a particular industry.

If the objective of the policy is to maintain minimum production and/or employment level, then a strong argument can be made that this is best achieved via quantity restriction (i.e., quota). The reason is that the quantity restrictions limit units imported from the rest of the world and thereby effectively guarantee a given amount of the domestic market to domestic suppliers. In contrast, price restrictions (i.e., tariffs) only preserve a differential between domestic prices and foreign prices without guaranteeing desired domestic productions and employment in the pro-

tected industry. In short, the quotas will protect the production and employment levels in the industry, irrespective of the business cycle
conditions. Although, in principle, tariffs could provide an equivalent protection, the tariff rate would have to be adjusted over the business cycle.
This would clearly raise the administrative cost of the tariff program. On
the other hand, since the restrictions are usually of a temporary nature,
the quotas will not need any adjustment during the period in which they
are in effect. Thus a strong argument can be made that administratively,
the quotas will be less expensive to implement.

Whether the imposition of trade restrictions aimed at protecting individual industries results in retaliatory actions by the rest of the world
depends on whether the U.S. convinces the rest of the world that the actions taken fall under the GATT escape clause. If unsuccessful, then the
rest of the world's first step in the retaliation process usually follows the
GATT guidelines. The affected countries will counter with restrictions
affecting an equal value of that country's export from the U.S. Thus, the
costs of retaliatory measures will not be borne directly by the protected
industry. Some other U.S. producers or perhaps consumers will be most
affected.

THE DETERMINANTS OF ACROSS-THE-BOARD
RESTRICTIONS: THE MACROEVENTS

The analysis in this book identifies via empirical analysis macro-and
microconditions conducive to protectionist policies. The analysis of the
macroevents shows that a deterioration of the U.S. trade balance is associated with an across-the-board rise in protectionism in the U.S. This
relationship is explained, in part, by the mercantilist belief that a deterioration of the trade balance is paramount to exporting jobs to the rest of
the world. However, when carried to its logical extreme, this line of
reasoning suggests that since the U.S. trade balance is negative, a restriction that resulted in autarky would increase U.S. employment—a highly
questionable implication.

Whether a deterioration of the trade balance signals a decline or an
increase in economic activity is an issue investigated in Chapter 7 of this
book. The results reported indicate that a deteriorating trade balance more
often than not signals an increase in economic activity and hence employment. The relationship between the trade balance and economic activity,
and that of protectionist policies and the trade balance point to a fairly

interesting and curious finding. Even though a deteriorating trade balance may signal an expanding economy, the rise in protectionism associated with a deteriorating trade balance could ultimately choke off the expansion. In this case jobs would be lost as the trade balance improved. In fact some writers have attributed the Great Depression to the protectionist policies leading to the Smoot-Hawley tarriffs.

An implication of the protectionist logic is that the imposition of across-the-board trade restrictions results in an improvement in the trade balance. However, there are solid theoretical arguments (e.g., Lerner's symmetry theorem) that lead one to question the theoretical relationship between the trade balance and trade restrictions.[1]

The empirical evidence reported in this book fails to uncover any causal relationship between effective tarriff rates and the trade balance. The results lead one to question the logic implicit in the view that a deterioration of the trade balance is analogous to exporting jobs away from the U.S.[2] Furthermore, the direct test of the relationship between trade actions and the overall employment level in the U.S. economy failed to uncover a significant relationship. In spite of the lack of empirical support for this proposition, the analysis reported in this book points to the pervasiveness and political appeal of this mercantilist proposition. Thus it is not surprising to find elected officials being sensitive to the desires of the electorate and thereby adopting protectionist macropolicies when the trade balance deteriorates.

THE DETERMINANTS OF INDUSTRY-SPECIFIC TRADE POLICIES: THE MICROEVENTS

The results reported in this study do not find any evidence, at the industry level, that imports give rise to protectionist policies. In contrast to the macroevents, the results indicate that declines in industry employment and/or industry profits relative to the national economy do exert a positive and significant effect on protectionism. These results are consistent with the view that trade restrictions may preserve the salary and profit levels of the protected industry. Thereby irrespective of the nature of foreign competition (i.e., fair or unfair), it is in the best interest of the industry workers and capitalists to lobby for relief from foreign competition. We have identified an issue of common interest to both capital and labor where the two groups willingly cooperate, rather than have the usually assumed adversary relationship.

The data used in the microevents measure the individual industries and stock performance relative to the national economy. The use of relative performance eliminates the effects of secular trends, stages of the business cycles, etc., that tend to have a common effect across industries. By contrast, the data used in the macroevents use aggregate data without adjusting for secular trend and/or business cycle conditions. This may, in part, explain the lack of a significant relationship between protectionism and employment or between protectionism and the stock market performance. Similarly, a strong argument can be made that the trade balance is the result of business cycle fluctuations and does not suffer from the potential problems that may affect the other two macrovariables. The theoretical analysis presented in this study argues that a country's trade balance tends to deteriorate when its economy grows faster than the rest of the world's. That is, if a country is growing at an above average rate, it tends to acquire more goods and services that it produces. The net imports of goods and services are exchanged for further claims (bonds and stocks) against the output of the economy. Since the deterioration of a country's trade balance is related to the economic performance of the country relative to the world economy, the analysis implicitly removes the effects of variables that generate a common effect on the performance of the national economies. This analysis suggests that the macrolevel-appropriate framework of analysis is that of an integrated world economy where the analysis focuses on the performance of an individual country relative to the world economy.[3]

EFFECTS OF INDUSTRY-SPECIFIC TRADE RESTRICTIONS

Import restrictions, if effective, afford some protection to the various industries. The restrictions also create benefit to those able to circumvent the restrictions. In some instances foreign producers take advantage of existing loopholes within the law, as was the case in the color TV industry, where manufacturers took advantage of U.S. law and reimported unfinished sets. The net effect was a circumvention of the restriction, at a cost of 5 percent tax on value added. Other times the circumvention is not so simple and easy. For example the restriction in tonnage (VRA) on imported steel was partially offset through a change in the composition of steel imported by the U.S. Even though the total tonnage declined, the value of the tonnage increased by approximately 30 percent. That is, the rest of the world minimized the effect of the quotas by altering the composition and shifting toward the higher-valued (higher profit margin) steel. In addition, countries not subject to the restraints were able to increase their export to the U.S. market. Once again, trade restrictions failed to deliver their promise of a healthier domestic steel industry. Historically, the steel restrictions have been like a rock in the middle of a river. The world supply of steel simply moved around the restrictions much as water moves around an obstacle that only partially blocks its flow. Trade patterns shifted without significantly altering the location of steel production. There is a swirl of distortion at the point of interference, but little is changed downstream.

The steel industry's response has been to ultimately ask for the equivalent of a dam to be placed across the river of imports, regulating the flow of steel into the U.S. regardless of its source. The recent ITC's recommendations would attempt to achieve precisely that result. Such a comprehensive policy, if skillfully designed and competently administered, could change the flow of steel mill products into the U.S. Even in this case, however, it is far from clear that the steel industry would be better off. The more successful the restriction is in isolating the U.S. market from the world steel market, the greater the incentives to cut new channels of distribution for foreign steel. Possible ways of circumventing the restriction will be through the import of semifinished steel. However, the ITC is already aware of this channel and has recommended that a 15 percent tariff be imposed on imports of semifinished steel in excess of 1.5 million tons. Another possible channel of circumvention is through the increase in the imports of fabricated steel. For example, the Los Angeles-based Don Walker Corp., the nation's largest independent, is considering moving some of its manufacturing operation to Canada. Such a facility would be able to use the inexpensive imported steel. In this way, Walker could continue to sell its steel products in the U.S. at prices competitive with foreign suppliers.[4] This kind of effort to get around the steel import restrictions already has been labeled "downstream dumping" by those who would curtail imports of all kinds. The lesson is clear: Protectionism creates incentives to circumvent the trade restrictions. To the extent that resources are unnecessarily spent, then the economy as a whole will be worse off.

The results reported in this book suggest that the industry-specific, microrestrictions failed to improve the stock performance, and in most cases had a negative and significant effect. Similarly, with the exception of the steel industry, the trade restriction appears to have an insignificant effect in the industry employment performance, and the insignificant results consistent with ineffective protectionist policies where circumvention is fairly easy to achieve. In addition, the negative and significant results are consistent with an ineffective policy where circumvention is largely effective, but costly. A positive and significant result is consistent with a protectionist policy where circumvention is fairly costly. It is very fitting that the positive and significant results occur in the steel industry. Where the different restrictions have been steadily blocking the flow of steel into the U.S., the results suggest that the U.S. steel industry may have finally built the dam that will prevent the inflow of steel. However, the cost of constructing the dam may very well exceed the benefits achieved. Notice that while the restrictions may have arrested the decline in employment, they have not arrested the decline in profitability. Finally, to the extent that other domestic producers, such as the domestic automakers, have to use the now more expensive steel, their products will also become less competitive.

The historical trade restrictions aimed at helping a particular industry have been of a temporary nature. The usual justification for the restriction is to provide breathing room to the industry while it modernizes. Once the restriction is granted, then the industry must decide whether to really attempt to modernize or to go along with some modernization and continue demand for protection. The decision depends in part on which one is most profitable to the industry. To the extent that modernization of plant facilities is not really viable, then resources will be directed against market forces and the lobbying for protectionist policies will become increasingly more expensive. Interestingly, it is in those industries that the successive protectionist policies will reduce the flow of imports, while the policies may in fact arrest the decline in employment. The necessary investment flow to modernize the industry plants will not be forthcoming.

In contrast to the policymakers, investors in those endangered industries recognize that their industries have become uneconomical and attempt to minimize their losses by asking for protection. They also recognize that the industry may no longer be viable under the given structure. The labor force is faced with a somewhat similar problem. Saddled with industry-specific human capital, to seek employment in other industries will entail a significant loss of salary. Thus, faced with this choice, seeking a new job at a lower pay or lobbying for protectionist policies that will preserve their higher salary, the choice is clear. Workers will be willing to spend a significant amount of resources to lobby for protectionist legislation. For capital owners in the industry, the problem is somewhat similar for capital in place. However, the choice is completely different when choosing to invest (add new capital to the industry). This explains in part why industry employment performance may be more closely connected with protectionist pressures than the industry stock return performance. It may also explain why investment has been below expectation in the industry for which protectionist policies have been successful in arresting the decline in employment. The political response to continued protection of the industry in the face of the lack of profit reinvestment is to insist that in return for protection from foreign competition, the industry must submit its capital budget to the treasury for approval. This approach to trade policy would clearly open the door for a national "industrial policy."

"RENT-SEEKING" BEHAVIOR BY U.S. TRADE PARTNERS

The imposition of trade restrictions will also give rise to "rent-seeking" behavior on the part of foreign governments. To the extent that resources are spent on these activities, the rest of the world will also be made worse off. For example, in the 1979–81 base period chosen by the ITC and U.S. administration, proposed reduction of foreign producers' share of the U.S. market clearly favors the Japanese and European producers. One would expect the Latin American countries to object to the allocation of these steel quotas and to argue that their ability to service their foreign debt and to maintain democratic institutions requires added consideration in the form of somewhat higher quotas. Within two days after the ITC announced its recommendation, Argentina was asking for a quota larger than recommended by the ITC. In short, the developing nations were quite willing to cooperate in the cartelization of the U.S. steel market, as long as they received their share of the extra profits created by the cartel.

THE OUTLOOK FOR TRADE POLICY

The evidence presented in this book suggests that political considerations determine, in part, many of the U.S. trade policies. The recent decisions by President Reagan may very well suggest the path of trade policy for the remainder of the decade. At issue is whether the administration will flirt with the policies of protectionism or devise a strategy to counter the protectionists. The risk of flirtation is entrapment. Protectionism is seductive in its promise of saving American jobs. But the promise is a false one.

Protectionist policies enjoy considerable support in Congress. Of particular concern is the protectionist sentiment among the Republican leaders in the Senate. For example, the majority whip, Alan Simpson of Wyoming, was cosponsor of the Simpson-Mazzoli bill. The new Chairman of the Senate Commerce Committee, James Danforth of Missouri, is a cosponsor of the "local content bill" which would effectively eliminate foreign base competition to the domestic auto industry. The chairman of the Republican senatorial campaign committee, John Heinz of Pennsylvania, has been an open advocate of restriction on steel imports. Finally, the chairman of the Republican Conference, John Chafee of Rhode Island, is an advocate of government intervention.

The position of the Republican leadership in the Senate suggests that protectionist forces will remain fairly influential for the remainder of the decade. Thus the problems for advocates of free trade will be to keep protectionist pressures within bounds and to avoid repeating the experience of the Smoot-Hawley act of 1930.

Ironically, the growing push for protectionism is due in part to the success of the Reagan administration economic program. This book documents empirically that pressures for trade restrictions arise when the trade balance deteriorates. However, a later chapter argues that simultaneously, a country's trade balance deteriorates and its capital account improves when its economy grows faster than the rest of the world's. It is precisely this phenomenon that has been ignited by the Reagan tax cuts.

U.S. and non-U.S. investors alike have responded to the U.S. tax cuts. Investment in the U.S. economy increased substantially. Foreign investors have also participated in this growth economy as manifested by a positive U.S. capital balance.

The improved capital account and simultaneous deterioration of the U.S. trade balance is the result of the strength of the U.S. economy. A symptom of this strength is that U.S. industrial production and employment gains during 1983 outrank by wide margins the gains posted in other industrial countries.

Other factors outside a federal policy will prove to have a positive effect on the U.S. economy. These include a second realization of a significant decline in oil prices that is directly related to the U.S. decontrol of natural gas prices. The 1981 decline in prices is directly related to the oil policies implemented in 1981. The effects of these policies have been to increase the overall supply of energy in the U.S. as well as to increase the price elasticity of the U.S. import function. OPEC appears to have neglected the effect of decontrol on its market power.[5] Over 1983–84 OPEC could be characterized as placing a large bet on seeing the demand for its oil rise along with the strong U.S. recovery and the shift toward economic growth in the rest of the industrialized world. But it is now clear to OPEC and its customers that the bet has been lost. Between 1982 and the first half of 1984, world oil consumption increased only 900,000 barrels a day to 53.9 million barrels. This was more than met by non-OPEC supplies as OPEC oil production fell 900,000 barrels a day to 17.8 million barrels.

The U.S. economy will benefit directly from the fall in oil prices. Those industries intensive in the use of energy—such as utilities or those products that use energy such as the auto industry—will do particularly well. The decline in energy prices will affect differentially the demand for large, as opposed to small, and high- as opposed to low-performance automobiles. To the extent that the U.S. automobiles capture a larger share of the large automobile market than the foreign automakers, the change in the composition of demand will fall disproportionately on U.S. automakers. Therefore, employment in the auto and related industries should increase as a result of the fall in energy prices. The increase in the employment and profit performance of these industries located in the "rust belt," will result in a decline in industry-specific protectionist pressures.

NOTES

1. A clear exception being the corner solution where the economy was initially experiencing a trade balance deficit and the trade action resulted in autarky.

2. The lack of a relationship between protectionist policies and the growth in employment in the U.S. economy may be partly explained by the fact that the empirical analysis did not adjust for the stage of the business cycle. On the other hand, one can argue that the trade balance more adequately reflects the stages of the business cycle, in which case the balance would be proxying for employment. Although this is an interesting hypothesis, no attempts were made to discriminate between this hypothesis and the one developed in the text.

3. Due to lack of data (e.g., foreign stocks total returns), no attempts were made to relate U.S. employment and stock returns relative to the world economy, to protectionist policies in the U.S.

4. See Tumulty (1984).

5. The effect of oil and gas decontrol are discussed in a series of papers by Bollman, Canto and Melich (1982) and Canto (1982).

Bibliography

Alexander, S. "The Effect of Devaluation on a Trade Balance." IMF Staff papers II, no. 2 (April 1950):263–78.

Allen, F. "Executives Say Imports Pose Serious Threat." *Wall Street Journal,* August 27, 1980, p. 17.

Amemiya, T. "Qualitative Response Models: A Survey." *Journal of Economic Literature* 19, no. 4 (December 1981):1483–1536.

Annual Statistical Report. American Iron and Steel Institute (Washington, D.C. 1981).

Bahree, B. "Bilateral Trade Accords are Blasted by Head of GATT in Appeal for Unity." *Wall Street Journal,* August 20, 1981, p. 34.

Beaver, W.H. "Econometric Properties of Alternative Security Return Methods." *Journal of Accounting Research* 19, no. 1 (Spring 1981):163–83.

Becker, G. "A Theory of the Allocation of Time." *Economic Journal* 75 (1965):493–517.

Bhagwati, J. N. and B. Hansen. "A Theoretical Analysis of Smuggling." *Quarterly Journal of Economics* 87, no. 2 (May 1973):172–87.

Bhagwati, J. N. and T. N. Srinivasan. "Smuggling and Trade Policy." *Journal of Public Economics* 2 (November 1973):377–89.

Bhagwati, J. N. and T.N. Srinivasan. "Revenue Seeking: A Generalization of the Theory of Tariffs." *Journal of Political Economy* 88, no. 6 (December 1980):1069–87.

Bollman, G.W., V. A. Canto, and K. A. Melich. "Oil Decontrol: The Power of Incentives." *Oil and Gas Journal* 80, no. 2 (January 11, 1982):92–101.

Break, George F. "The Incidence and Economic Effects of Taxation." In *The Economics of Public Finance.* Washington: The Brookings Institute, 1974.

Brock, W. A. and S. P. Magee. "The Economics of Special Interest Politics: The Case of the Tariff." *American Economic Review Papers and Proceedings* 68 (May 1978):246–50.

Brock, W., S. Magee, and L. Young. "The Progressivity of Endogenous Tariff Policy in General Equilibrium." In V. Canto and K. Dietrich, *Industrial Policy and International Trade.* JAI Press, forthcoming 1985.

Brown, K., L. Lockwood, and S. Summer. "On Examinations of Event Dependency and Structural Change in Securities Price Models." June 1983, mimeograph.

Brown, S. and G. Warner. "Using Daily Stock Returns in Event Studies." Working paper, February 1983. University of Rochester.

Canto, V. A., R. V. Eastin, A. B. Laffer, and J. C. Turney. "The Effects of Trade Restrictions on the U. S. Economy." A. B. Laffer Associates (March 15, 1982).

Canto, V. A. "The United States Fuel Use Patterns: The Outlook for the 1980s." *Oil and Gas Journal* 80, no. 34 (August 23, 1982):125–43.

Canto, V. A., A. B. Laffer, and J. C. Turney. "Trade Policy and the U.S. Economy." *Financial Analysts Journal* 38, no. 5 (September–October 1982):27–46.

Canto, V. A. and K. Melich. "Natural Gas Decontrol: The Road to Lower Energy Prices." *Public Utility Fortnightly* 100, no. 9 (October 28, 1982):31–39.

Canto, V. A., R. V. Eastin, and A. B. Laffer. "Failure of Protectionism: A Study of the Steel Industry." *Columbia Journal of World Business* 17, no. 4 (Winter 1982):43–57.

Canto, V. A., D. H. Joines, and A. B. Laffer. *Foundations of Supply Side Economics.* New York: Academic Press, 1983.

Canto, V. A. and R. Webb. "Persistent Growth Rate Differentials Among States in a National Economy with Factor Mobility." In V. A. Canto, D. Joines and A. Laffer (eds.), *Foundations of Supply Side Economics.* New York: Academic Press, 1983.

Canto, V. A. and A. B. Laffer. "The Effectiveness of Orderly Marketing Agreements: The Color T.V. Case." *Business Economics* 18, no. 1 (January 1983):38–45.

Canto, V. A. "The Effects of Voluntary Restraint Agreements: A Case Study of the Steel Industry." *Applied Economics* 16, no. 2 (April 1984):175–86.

Carey, S. "U.S. Steel Plans to Cite 5 Nations in Trade Actions." *Wall Street Journal,* February 9, 1984, p. 4.

Christie, A. "On Information Arrival and Hypothesis Testing." 1983, mimeograph.

"Commerce Finds Subsidies in Steel Investigations." *Commerce News,* U.S. Department of Commerce, International Trade Commission (June 11, 1982):1a–3a.

Cooper, R. "An Assessment of Currency Devaluation in Developing Countries." In G. Rainis (ed.), *Government and Economic Development.* New Haven: Yale University Press, 1971, pp. 472–515.

Craig, G. A. "A Monetary Approach to the Balance of Trade." *American Economic Review* 71, no. 3 (June 1981):460–66.

Crandall, R. *The U.S. Steel Industry in Recurrent Crisis.* Washington: The Brookings Institution, 1981.

1980 Economic Report of the President.

The Effect of the Tokyo Round of Multilateral Trade Negotiations on the U.S. Economy; an updated view. The Congress of the United States, Congressional Budget Office (July 1979).

Falvey, R. E. "A Note on Preferential and Illegal Trade Under Quantitative Restrictions." *Quarterly Journal of Economics* 92, no. 1 (February 1978).

Fama, E., M. Jensen Fisher, and R. Roll. "The Adjustment of Stock Prices to New Information." *International Economic Review* 10, no. 1 (Feburary 1969):1–21.

Farnsworth, C. H. "Added Steel Complaints Threatened." *New York Times,* February 9, 1984a, p. 31.

Farnsworth, C. "Panel Asks Protection for Steel." *New York Times,* June 13, 1984b, p. 1.

Fialka, J. "Pledges by Mondale Add Up to a Big Bill, An Analysis Suggests." *Wall Street Journal,* January 24, 1984, p. 1.

"U.S.S.R. Buys Superphosphoric Acid from Belgium." *Fertilizer International,* no. 37 (November 1981):1.

"U.S.S.R. Signs Protocol Arrangement." *Foreign Trade* (February 1981).

Frenkel, J. and H. Johnson. *The Monetary Approach to the Balance of Payments.* Toronto: University of Toronto Press, 1976.

Granger, C. "Investigating Causal Relations by Econometric Models and Cross Spectral Methods." *Econometrica* 37, no. 3 (July 1969):424–38.

Greenhouse, S. "EEC Retaliation List Against U.S. Disclosed." *New York Times,* January 12, 1984a, p. 27.

Greenhouse, S. "Bethlehem Steel Seeks Import Bar." *New York Times,* January 25, 1984b, p. 1.

Houthakker, H. and S. Magee. "Income and Price Elasticities in World Trade." *Review of Economics and Statistics* 51, no. 2 (May 1969):111–25.

International Financial Statistics Yearbook. International Monetary Fund, Washington, D.C.

Jain, A. "The Behavior of Industrial Stock Indices—1932–1982." Ph.D. dissertation, 1985 (expected). University of Southern California.

Kilborn, P. "Not Much Time Left To Resolve Deficits, Volcker Tells House." *New York Times*, February 8, 1984, p. 1.

Krueger, A. O. "The Political Economy of the Rent-Seeking Society." *American Economic Review* 64, no. 3 (June 1974):291–303.

Lachica, E. and G. Sieb. "Agencies Vie Over Exports in Technology." *Wall Street Journal*, February 2, 1984, p. 33.

Lachica, E. and T. Boyle. "ITC Proposes Quotas, Tariffs on Steel Imports." *Wall Street Journal*, July 12, 1984, p. 3.

Laffer, A. B. and M. Miles. *International Economics in an Integrated World.* Glenview, IL: Scott, Foresman, 1981.

Lavergne, R. *The Political Economy of U.S. Tariffs: An Empirical Analysis.* New York: Academic Press, 1983.

Lerner, A. "The Symmetry Between Import and Export Taxes." *Economica* 3, no. 11 (August 1936):306–13.

LeRoy, S. "Expectation Models of Asset Prices: A Survey of Theory." *The Journal of Finance* 37 (March 1982):185–217.

Lohr, S. "Japanese Plan Stirs Computer Concerns." *New York Times*, January 18, 1984, p. 22.

"Brock Calls for Fair Foreign Trade; Moves Close to Endorsing 'Reciprocity' Between Nations." *Los Angeles Times*, February 2, 1982, p. 2.

Magee, S. "Prices, Incomes, and Foreign Trade." In P. Kenen (ed.), *International Trade and Finance: Frontiers for Research.* New York: Cambridge University Press, 1975.

Martin, D. "Fishermen in U.S. Angered by Canada." *New York Times*, January 16, 1984, p. 19.

Masulis, R. "The Effect of Capital Structure Change on Security Prices: A Study of Exchange Offers."*Journal of Financial Economics* 8 (June 1980):139–77.

McLure, C. E. "Taxation, Substitution and Industrial Location." *Journal of Political Economy* 78, no. 1 (Jan/Feb. 1970):112–32.

Meade, J. *The Theory of International Economic Policy, Vol. I: The Balance of Payments.* London: Oxford University Press, 1951.

Merton, R. "On Estimating the Expected Return in the Market: On Exploratory Investigation." NBER Working Paper No. 444, February 1980.

Miles, M. "The Effects of Devaluation on the Trade Balance and Balance of Payments: Some New Results." *Journal of Political Economy* 87, no. 3 (June 1979):600–19.

Mundell, R. "International Trade and Factor Mobility." *American Economic Review* 47, no. 3 (1957):321–25.

Mussa, M. "Dynamic Adjustment in the Heckscher–Ohlin–Samuelson Model." *Journal of Political Economy* 86, no. 5 (Oct 1978):775–91.

"U.S. Trade Bar Angers Europeans." *New York Times*, January 23, 1984, p. 1.

"Shoe-Import Quotas Asked." *New York Times*, January 24, 1984, p. 23.

"Chrysler Backs Steel Quota Bill." *New York Times,* June 12, 1984, p. 16.

Orcutt, G. "Measurement of Price Elasticities in International Trade." *Review of Economics and Statistics* 36, no. 2(1950):117–32.

Pasztos, A. "Sharp Boost in Duties on Foreign Trucks is not Expected to Aid Sales of U.S. Models." *Wall Street Journal,* August 20, 1980, p. 9.

Pine, A. "GATT Director Doubts Imports Safeguard Can Be Agreed on at Next World Trade Session." *Wall Street Journal,* October 8, 1982, p. 36.

Pine, A. "GATT Talks Face Problems as Negotiators Fail to Agree on Any Big Issue on Agenda." *Wall Street Journal,* November 25, 1982c, p. 5.

Pine, A. "Ministers Mull World Trade Nov. 24." *Wall Street Journal,* November 16, 1982b, p. 37.

Pine, A. "GATT Meeting Communique Isn't Likely to Have Much Influence on World Trade." *Wall Street Journal,* November 30, 1982d, p. 2.

Pine, A. "U.S. Worries That Nov. 24 GATT Parley Will Increase Protectionism Not Trade." *Wall Street Journal,* November 5, 1982a, p. 36.

Pine, A. "Brazil Orange Juice Products Hurt Firms in U.S., Panel Finds." *Wall Street Journal,* August 26, 1983, p. 38.

Pine, A. "How President Came to Favor Concessions for U.S. Textile Makers." *Wall Street Journal,* January 6, 1984a, p. 1.

Pine, A. "Reagan Vows to Seek Voluntary Steel Import Curbs." *Wall Street Journal,* September 19, 1984b, p. 3.

Ray, E. J. "The Determinants of Tarriffs and Non-tarriff Trade Restrictions in the United States." *Journal of Political Economy* 89, no. 1 (February 1981):105–21.

Ruback, R. "The Effect of Price Controls on Equity Values." WPS—MERCF2-06, December 1979. University of Rochester.

Salant, M. "Devaluations Improve the Balance of Payments Even if Not the Trade Balance." In P. Clark, D. Logue, and R. Sweeney (eds.), *The Effects of Exchange Rate Adjustments.* OASIA research, Department of the Treasury, U.S. Government Printing Office, Washington, D.C., 1977.

Samuelson, P. A. "International Trade and the Equalization of Factor Prices." *Economic Journal* 58 (1948):163–84.

Samuelson, P. "International Factor–Price Equalization Once Again." *Economic Journal* 59 (1949):181–97.

Samuelson, P. A. "Equalization by Trade of the Interest Rate Along with the Real Wage." In Baldwin et al., *Trade Growth and the Balance of Payments.* Chicago: Rand McNally, 1965, pp. 35–52.

Sieb, G. "Reagan Sends Caribbean Plan to Congress. Weak Economy Threatens Full Support." *Wall Street Journal,* March 18, 1982, p. 5.

Straus, R. "The Mercantilist Threat to World Trade." *Wall Street Journal,* November 24, 1982, p. 26.

Suh, J. "Voluntary Export Restraints and their Effect on Exporters and Consumers: The Case of Footwear Quotas." Working paper 71, Center for the Study of American Business, October 1981. Washington University, St. Louis.

Tharp, M. "U.S. Now Able to Export More Beef and Oranges to Japan Under New Farm-Trade Pact." *Wall Street Journal,* December 6, 1978, p. 38.

Tumulty, K. "State Steel Processors Say Import Curbs May Force Them to Leave." *Los Angeles Times,* December 13, 1984, p. 1.

"The U.S. Auto Industry Status Report." U.S. Department of Commerce, December 1981.

Vicker, R. "U.S.-Common Market Agree to Reduce Tariff Affecting $2 Billion Annual Trade." *Wall Street Journal*, January 17, 1962, p. 3.

Vinocur, J. "French Minister Urges Steps to Curb Flight of Europe's Capital to the U.S." *New York Times*, January 15, 1984, p. 8.

"Common Market Raises Tariffs on Some U.S. Goods Effective Today." *Wall Street Journal*, August 1, 1962, p. 4.

"Refusal of the Common Market to Cut Tariffs on U.S. Poultry May Prompt Retaliation." *Wall Street Journal*, July 31, 1963, p. 8.

"The Attractions of Quotas." *Wall Street Journal*, January 15, 1969, p. 18.

"Benzenoid Chemical Tariff Cuts Postponed." *Wall Street Journal*, December 16, 1969, p. 33.

"EEC Warns of Reprisals." *Wall Street Journal*, October 13, 1970, p. 2.

"Economists Warn Peril of SST if Trade Bill Passes." *Wall Street Journal*, November 19, 1970, p. 3.

"Trade Bill Foes Lose Hard Fight on Amendment." *Wall Street Journal*, November 19, 1970, p. 3.

"House Approves Controversial Trade Measure." *Wall Street Journal*, November 20, 1970, p. 4.

"Japan Cabinet Formally Cuts Tariffs on Some Imports 20 Percent." *Wall Street Journal*, November 20, 1970, p. 10.

"Japan Will Reduce Tariff on 30 Items, Eliminate Import Quota on Four More." *Wall Street Journal*, December, 1970.

"Common Market Levy on Import of Oranges from U.S. to Be Cut." *Wall Street Journal*, June 1, 1971, p. 18.

"Japan's Cabinet Bows to U.S. Request. End Nine-Year Buy-Japanese Rule." *Wall Street Journal*, September 12, 1972, p. 14.

"EEC to Reinstate Cheese-Export Subsidies and U.S. Gears Up for Battle Once More." *Wall Street Journal*, February 17, 1975, p. 20.

"European Soybean Tax Could Widely Damage Relations, U.S. Warns." *Wall Street Journal*, July 12, 1976, p. 7.

"Japan Lifts Import Ban on Some Grapefruit From U.S." *Wall Street Journal*, April 5, 1977, p. 6.

"U.S. Ruling Faults Imports of Korean Bicycle Tires." *Wall Street Journal*, March 23, 1979, p. 36.

"Reaganites Plan Trade Offensive to Prod Europe, Japan to Admit More U.S. Goods." *Wall Street Journal*, January 5, 1982.

"Steel Firms Will File Unfair-Trade Cases; Upheaval Seen in Markets for Some Time." *Wall Street Journal*, January 11, 1982, p. 2.

"U.S. Weighs Trade Actions Against Japan." *Wall Street Journal*, February 9, 1982, p. 3.

"U.S. Plans for Duties on Some Steel Imports May Provide Little Help to Domestic Firms." *Wall Street Journal*, June 14, 1982, p. 4.

"Commerce Unit Says Six Nations 'Dumping' Steel." *Wall Street Journal*, August 11, 1982, p. 3.

"U.S. Rules European Steel Prices Unfair; Duties as High as 26 Percent May Be Imposed." *Wall Street Journal,* August 26, 1982 p. 3.

"Europe Agrees To Cut Steel Exports to the U.S." *Wall Street Journal,* October 22, 1982, p. 3.

"EC's Retaliation on Steel Curbs Disappoints U.S." *Wall Street Journal,* January 16, 1984, p. 23.

"U.S.-Canada Talks Break Down on Treaty for Salmon Fishing." *Wall Street Journal,* January 30, 1984, p. 46.

"U.S. Tentatively Rules 3 Countries Subsidize Various Steel Exports." *Wall Street Journal,* February 8, 1984, p. 17.

Wannisky, J. *The Way the World Works.* New York: Basic Books, 1978.

Index

absorption approach, 154, 160
across-the-board protectionist policies,
    132, 188, 189
agricultural fund for price support, 28
American Selling Price, 29, 30
antidumping laws, 30
antidumping policies, 5, 8
average prediction error (APE), 140

"beggar-thy-neighbor" policies, 16
Bethlehem Steel Corp., 125
bilateral agreement, 2
breathing room, 40, 43, 188
Bretton Woods, 3, 7
Burke-Hartke bill, 5, 6
business cycle, 189

Caribbean Basin Initiative, 12
circumvention of Orderly Marketing
    Agreements, 78
circumvention of restrictions, 191, 193
countervailing and penalty duties: steel,
    11, 96, 101
countervailing duties, 10, 28, 32, 106,
    138
countervailing duty petitions: steel, 96
country-specific equilibrium, 166, 168
cumulative average prediction error
    (CAPE), 140, 142, 144, 148
Customs Valuation Code, 5

decontrol of oil and gas, 195, 196
devaluation and the trade balance, 158,
    159
downstream dumping, 192
dumping, 10, 88, 101, 106
dumping charges, 96, 97, 98, 101

elasticity approach, 154
embargo, 35, 36
    motivation, 115
effects of embargoes on:

alternative suppliers, 116
choice of commodity, 40
economic efficiency, 43
factor prices, 38, 40
investment, 41
migration, 38
mobile factors, 38
patterns of trade, 39, 116
product prices, 41
production, 40
protection, 40
standard of living, 40
U.S. supplies of superphosphoric acid
    (SPA), 115, 118
USSR production of superphosphoric
    acid, 117, 118
employment of protectionism, 190
event methodology, 139

factor price equalization, 163, 167
"fair" competition, 8
fair trade, 1, 32, 132, 185, 186
foreign vs. domestic cars, 108
free trade, 1, 12, 29, 186
full income, 164, 165

General Agreement of Tariffs and Trade
    (GATT), 3, 5, 7, 8, 10, 12, 13, 23,
    28, 29, 32, 132
    basic goals, 3
    escape clause, 187, 189
    ministerial meetings, 12, 16
global economy, 153
global equilibrium, 166
global quotas, 105
    on raw steel, 107
gold convertibility, 7

household commodity, 162

import injury, 186
incidence of a tax, 36

201

About The Author

Dr. Victor A. Canto received a B.Sc. from M.I.T. and an M.A. and Ph.D. in Economics from the University of Chicago.

He has been an Assistant Professor and an Associate Professor at the University of Southern California as well as Visiting Professor at the Universidad Central Del Este, Dominican Republic.

In addition to his academic position, Dr. Canto has been economics advisor to the Finance Minister of the Dominican Republic, economist for the economics studies division of the Dominican Republic Central Bank, as well as a consultant to Puerto Rico's Treasury and Government Financial Council.

Dr. Canto's other books include *Foundations of Supply Side Economics* and *Apuntaciones Sobre Inflación y Politica Economica en Republica Dominicana*. His publications have appeared in the *Economic Inquiry, Southern Economic Journal, Public Finance, Journal of International Money And Finance*, and the *Journal of Macroeconomics*, among others.